D1571322

The Plot to Destroy Israel

The Plot to Destroy Israel

The Road to Armageddon

by

Alvin Rosenfeld

G. P. Putnam's Sons, New York

Second Impression

Copyright © 1977 by Alvin **Rosenfeld**

SBN: 399-11854-3

Library of Congress Catalog Card Number: 76-53660

PRINTED IN THE UNITED STATES OF AMERICA.

In memory of the beautiful and promising children of my friends in Israel who died, hating no one, at the hands of the killers of the dream,
And to Rita and Harry, with love.

Contents

The Plot to Destroy Israel

The Road to
Armageddon

Since 1948, the Arab states have been waging a savage and genocidal war against Israel. This war has erupted four times into raging confrontations which have themselves been called wars. It has, in a bloody detour, laid waste to the small and once progressive state of Lebanon. It has brought political terror to a new pitch of bestiality in the Palestinian paramilitary forces raised, trained, financed and unleashed by Israel's enemies, the sovereign states of the Middle East.

These states—Egypt, Syria, Libya, Jordan, Iraq, Saudi Arabia and an assembly of satellite countries—share a single, enduring goal: the elimination of Israel from the map and its replacement by an Arab, Islamic state, as their machinations in Lebanon graphically demonstrated. They are prepared to plunge the Middle East into hell in the pursuit of this goal; nothing is to be permitted to stand in the way of its satisfaction, not human life, not political responsibility, not the needs of the poor, not truth.

11

This book deals with fanaticism and brutality, with atrocity and race hate, with the crude anti-Semitism of Libya's Muammar el-Quaddafi and the slick anti-Semitism of Egypt's fickle Anwar el-Sadat. It deals with the lies the Arabs tell, the brazen fictions with which they cloak their intent to destroy Israel. It deals, too, with the weakness and gullibility of Israel's few friends among the nations and their failure to recognize that the Arabs feel no moral compunction to deal ethically with any peoples of the world.

This is not a work of undercover investigative reporting. Every fact in this book is available to any reporter diligent enough to search the records of the past years. All of these facts are known to every intelligence agency worth its salt. Some of the information in these pages comes from United States government transcripts open to any interested member of the public. Much of it is in shocking variance with the things we are being told by our own leaders and the things we accept as truth in news reports. Certainly, some of it has been deliberately buried, but most has simply been downplayed because it does not suit the climate of capitulation to Arab pressures throughout the world.

There are 150 million Arabs. They are massed against a single small state of 3 million souls. "Who will survive at the very end? The 3 million or the 150 million?" That question was asked of an American visitor to Cairo in 1975, by the Foreign Minister of Egypt.

Elementary decency demands that we do everything in our power to ensure that both the 3 million and the 150 million survive. In order to do that, we must first search the words and the acts of the people who are determined to see the 3 million perish—even if such an attempt on their part brings Armageddon in its wake.

1

Ⲧⲏⲉ Ⲙⲁⲥⲧⲉⲣ Ⲡⲗⲁⲛ

November 10, 1975. It was a grim and chilling day in New York. The United Nations General Assembly was sitting in judgment of one of its smaller member states. The Israeli delegation had absented itself in savage contempt from the UN chamber, but a flushed and excited group of Palestinian Arabs was on hand for the spectacle. By 72 to 35, with 32 abstentions, it was resolved that the United Nations General Assembly "determines that Zionism is a form of racism and racial discrimination." With that resolution, the Arab cabal in the UN had at last achieved what it had coveted for nearly three decades: a vote to "balance" the ballot by which the same body had welcomed Zionism as the national movement of the Jewish people and created the state which was to be known as Israel.

True, there was disgust in the UN chamber as well as triumph, and there was shame. Delegates of indigent countries were to confess afterward that they had auctioned their votes for Arab petrodollars. Delegates of countries vitally dependent on Middle Eastern oil were to admit that

13

they had given in to naked threats. There were embarrassed shrugs and red faces, downcast eyes and protestations of duress. In the corridors, men with ambassadorial titles detoured to avoid the accusing eyes of Israeli secretaries.

Who were the sponsors of the resolution which, in equating Zionism with racism, struck at the very foundations of the Jewish state? They included:

Saudi Arabia, an oil-rich desert oligarchy which does not have a single Jew resident within its borders, screens all visitors to ensure that Jews—with such rare and understandable exceptions as Henry Kissinger—do not enter the country and declines to do business with companies that employ Jews.

Egypt, governed by a single party whose leader, Anwar el-Sadat, has expressed extravagant admiration for Adolf Hitler.

Syria, a military dictatorship whose Jewish minority fled penniless to Israel, leaving a tiny, ghettoized remnant which is a model of abject humility.

Iraq, another provider of Jewish refugees to Israel, which is also involved in brutally suppressing its Kurdish minority.

Lebanon, a "confessional democracy" whose shaky balance of power between Christian and Moslem was even then being overturned by a civil war in which persons by the thousands were slain for no other reason than professing the wrong faith.

Libya, a theocracy whose military dictator recently augmented his house-to-house searches for empty liquor bottles (alcohol is proscribed in Islamic tradition) with the reimposition of the ancient Moslem law which penalizes thieves by chopping off their right hands.

Jordan, which banned Jews of all nationalities from its section of Jerusalem (which contained the Western or

Wailing Wall) during eighteen years of "stewardship" of the Old City.

Who voted willingly for the resolution? Its most vociferous supporters included:

The Soviet Union, whose Jewish citizens are mistrusted, harassed and required by law to carry cards identifying themselves as part of a race other than Russian.

Brazil, ruled by a junta of generals whose prisons echo with the screams of political prisoners being tortured.

Uganda, an African country of Byzantine bent, whose despotic leader, Idi Amin, eight months later welcomed the hijackers of an Air France jet diverted from the Tel Aviv-Paris run and graciously provided Ugandan troops to spell the terrorists at guarding the hostages.

All of these states, sponsors and supporters alike, swore that they had nothing against Israelis *as Jews*. It was "racism" alone that was on trial at the UN, they maintained.

In the long debate that stretched through the weeks before the actual vote, however, there were strange and ugly breaches in the anti-Zionist line. A mistrustful listener might even have suspected some of the speakers of animus toward something other than political Zionism. One of the more suspicious was Daniel Patrick Moynihan, then U.S. Ambassador to the United Nations.

"Not since [the Nazi war crimes' trials at] Nuremberg have you seen and heard such things as were being said during that debate," he told the *Washington Post* three months later. "That place was reeking with hate and violence."

One of the more strident anti-Zionists was a delegate of the Palestine Liberation Organization. Over the objections of the Israelis, who said he was a terrorist, he was on hand with Observer status, and ignoring the war of religions then building up in Lebanon, he forgot himself so far as to tell the UN Third Committee that Zionist theory was based on "expansion of the Jewish religion." He went on to compound the gaffe, to the manifest discomfort of some of his sponsors, who had not planned to mention Jews or Judaism at all. Jews could not live together with the citizens of the country in which they resided, nor could they belong to that country, he continued. Having delivered himself of that Himmlerian slur, the PLO Observer returned to the subject at hand, the racism of the Zionists. Zionists, he explained, tried to isolate Jews from the other peoples of the world and constituted the other face of anti-Semitism, since they tried to promote *Semitism.*

It went on like that, day in and day out, with an occasional disgusted objection from the delegates of the Western democracies. The Soviets concentrated on Israel as a bastion of imperialism and colonialist expansion. The Saudi Arabian ambassador issued a bombastic warning: "Wake up, you Zionists! I do not want to see a day of reckoning when your children, wives and loved ones will suffer inadvertently. You are closing your eyes to what might happen." The Arab representative of the Sudan, whose blacks have been slain by the thousands, referred to Israelis collectively as "the Zionist gang." The delegate of the pro-communist dictatorship that calls itself the People's Democratic Republic of Yemen described the Israelis as "Zionist gangsters."

These verbal distortions and threats, sinister as they were, might almost have seemed comical had it not been for the vote. The vote lent legitimacy, however spurious, to the ideological war against Israel. Suspect though its origins were, backed as it was by the least-respected members of the international community, forced through by blackmail and arm-twisting, it became a UN resolution, and the passage of a UN resolution labeling Zionism racism was clearly bad news. "Racism" is a knee-jerk word in the councils

16

of the United Nations. Its equation with Zionism had only one purpose—to render Israel a pariah among nations, as it has been a pariah in the Arab world since its founding.

Many years before, in pleading for the establishment of the Jewish state, the Zionist leader who was to become Israel's first president wryly described the classic Jew of the Diaspora as someone who carried anti-Semitism with him like a knapsack on his back. On November 10, 1975, the United Nations handed Chaim Weizmann's Israel a new knapsack.

Three days later, the PLO's al-Fatah planted a bomb in Zion Square in Jerusalem, killing seven teenagers and wounding and maiming scores of passers-by. The formula, according to a featured program on Damascus radio, was simple. "[The commandos] take one copy of the resolutions adopted by the UN, mix them with TNT and blow up Zion Square. . . . Now the resolutions . . . are turning into deeds."

In fact, the PLO and similar groups had never before required resolutions as a rationale for blowing people up. Long before anyone came up with the idea of stamping the Israelis as racists, there were tiny button bombs and booby-trapped candy bars in schoolyards in Jerusalem, grenades and bombs in supermarkets in Tel Aviv, bloodied and overturned school buses in the Galilee and bullets at the Munich Olympics.

To be sure, the UN resolution was a tool useful for internal Arab propaganda and valuable in conjunction with such acts as the bombing at Zion Square. Its true value, however, lay elsewhere. It was but a single step, a skirmish, a part of only one campaign in a vicious, wide-ranging and infinitely cunning war whose ultimate purpose is the obliteration of Israel.

Those who seek to erase Israel from the map are the

17

strangest of bedfellows. They are tribal sheikhs and urban Marxists, reactionary kinglets and radical Ba'ath socialists, oil lords and their subservient clients, monarchs and the dethroners of kings, stern authoritarians and men who live by violence and anarchy. Their lands stretch from the Atlantic Ocean to the Persian Gulf; their dialects are sometimes incomprehensible to one another; their political alliances shift and change like desert sands; they war upon one another or fawn upon one another; divided and often shrill with hatred, they speak with one voice against Israel. Even when they mercilessly shed each other's blood, as in Lebanon, they proclaim endless devotion to the cause of Palestine.

In keeping with their widely varied degrees of sophistication and the disparity of their resources, each of these belligerents functions differently in this conspiracy of destruction aimed at Israel. Some provide funds in the millions upon millions of dollars to arm others, finance terror, shore up insolvent "confrontation states," seduce neutrals and buy UN votes. Some provide men and machines which are used in those repeated instances when the war takes to the field, openly and at great human cost. Some heap largesse on grateful institutions in the West, move softly through the drawing rooms of diplomacy or invite figures of power to resplendent embassy parties.

They are men for all seasons, all ideologies, all eras. For the edification of the Third World, they are anti-colonialists seeking to eliminate an imperialist state. For the Africans, they are a new crusade against a white nation-state often erroneously compared with South Africa. For that portion of the American Black community which is itself anti-Semitic, they are victims of Jewish blockbusters. For Quakers, they are humanitarians looking only to return the dispossessed to their homeland. For Moslems, they are Mohammed's avenging army. For liberals, they are in search of a utopian state. For the meek, they are humble; for the devout, holy pilgrims to Jerusalem; for the poor, impoverished; and for the rich they are the endangered font of further riches.

Whatever their true motives, they have succeeded—by design, subconscious wish or accident—in postponing by at least thirty years the social and economic reforms so urgently needed in the Arab world. Crucial to this welcome by-product of the war against Israel is the issue of the hapless Palestinian refugees, through whom corrupt regimes have focused the passions of their own miserable masses upon a struggle beyond their borders. It is an irony that the scapegoat in this classic political diversion should be Israel; more than half of its population consists of refugees from Arab countries and their descendants and it is the only state in the Arab world that permits communists to run for office—and Israel's communists are a divisive and unpleasant group.

The Israeli communists and their rights cut no ice with the pragmatists in Moscow. The Soviet Union has chosen its allies in the Middle East by geopolitics rather than ideology. Russia's goals are eminently clear, as evidenced by the worrying presence of Soviet warships in the Mediterranean and the Red Sea. Wars of "national liberation," even wars waged by capitalists, theocrats and feudal lords, take precedence over social goals if the price is right. There are great spoils to be won in the Middle East which can be considered apart from national aspirations, whether of Arabs or of Jews: bases in Syria, air and sea lanes to the East and to Africa, a degree of control over oil supplies to the Western powers, a counterweight to American influence in the Eastern Mediterranean and the Persian Gulf, and more. So, Arab terrorists are housed in Moscow, arms from the USSR and its satellites are delivered to the Arabs without stint, wars are fought with the aid and counsel of the Soviets, and Russia's representatives work untiringly for the Arab cause on the diplomatic front.

The UN has long since become the Arabs' pliant instrument of war. It is no longer a parliament of man, but a collection of blocs making decisions for reasons of power and convenience, and both factors dictate support for the Arabs. Russian vetoes have guaranteed that the Security Council does not even mildly criticize Arab terror, though it rushes to condemn Israeli counterstrikes at terrorist bases and thereby manages, as the chief U.S. representative put it, to look "to effect and not to cause." A built-in majority—the twenty Arab states, the nineteen non-Arab countries in the Moslem bloc, the Russians and their stooges, the Third World adolescents seduced by Arab wealth and the cloying rhetoric of Arab anti-colonialism—assured the virtually automatic passage of scores of anti-Israel resolutions in other UN bodies, from the Human Rights Commission to the General Assembly.

The tone for the UN in the mid-1970s was set by, of all people, the Lebanese delegate to the United Nations Educational, Scientific and Cultural Organization (UNESCO) who blandly announced: "Israel is a state which belongs nowhere because it comes from nowhere." The Arab strategy was underlined by Egypt's Foreign Minister even as he negotiated with the State Department about "peace" in the Middle East: "It is inevitable that we escalate the campaign of isolating and rejecting Israel from the international community and from the UN." The flood of new resolutions inspired by the Arabs and dutifully rubberstamped by UN bodies had, in fact, a broader goal. These resolutions demanded that the Jewish state withdraw from "all the occupied territories" and stressed the "rights of the Palestinian people," but these ringing, libertarian

20

phrases were empty of real meaning, for the only Palestinians recognized either by the Arab belligerents or the UN were the extremists of the PLO, who had been voted official status in UN constituent agencies. There were no guarantees for Israel's sovereignty included in resolutions which would unleash thousands of hate-filled Arabs trained as guerrillas within the Jewish state. There are no promises of peace in exchange for Israeli relinquishment of control over the West Bank of the Jordan and the Gaza Strip. There was only the record, and the record showed that the people who so patiently and skillfully carried these measures to the floor of the UN were actually seeking only to destroy Israel diplomatically, economically and militarily.

The economic weapons, used to deprive Israel of markets and sources of goods and capital and designed to impoverish her and rob her of political allies, are coldly efficient. They are boycott and blockade, blacklist and blackmail, financial subversion and outright bribery. Oil, vital to the industrial and domestic well-being of Japan and the Western democracies, has been the most heavily publicized weapon in the arsenal. There are other, less evident ramifications. American companies, falling over one another in competition for fat contracts in new-rich Arab states, are induced to boycott Israel, join in a secondary boycott against firms which supply the Israelis, and screen Jews from their work forces. The Georgetown University School of Foreign Service, a traditional stepping-stone to the State Department, has received generous benefaction for the establishment of a center for the study of Arab society, courtesy of an ominous piece of philanthropy by a number of Arab countries and Mobil Oil. All is fair in commerce and war.

Nowhere in the world are nations arming more rapidly or spending more per capita on weapons than in the Arab countries dedicated to the obliteration of Israel. With American help and encouragement, Arab states are amassing vastly greater quantities of ultra-modern weaponry than Israel can buy or maintain. The Soviet Union has already armed the Syrians—and, in another incarnation, the Egyptians—with sophisticated devices capable of delivering missiles into the heart of Israel. Both great powers, conveniently ignoring past precedent, present stance and generic instability, have decided that certain Arab states are not combatants because they do not physically border on Israel. Thus, Russia has been pumping arms into Iraq and Libya without restraint as to quality or quantity, and the United States has been pouring weapons into Saudi Arabia and Kuwait.

Equally ominous, there is the Western assessment of some Arab belligerents directly on the battleline as "moderates" to be appeased with arms and defused with concessions wrung from Israel. Egypt, with a long record as the most active of the "confrontation states," is a notable case in point. In exchange for a sphinx-like silence instead of its customary threats to annihilate Israel, Egypt has begun to receive generous quantities of Western arms—and is encouraged to apply for more—to add to its enormous arsenal of Soviet war matériel for the next round.

Need there be a next round? Perhaps not, if the responsible nations of the world recognize the war against Israel in its unique totality and act to block its inexorable escalation. This would require a new look at the conflict and an acknowledgment of the hard fact that it is bounded by none of the strictures of "ethical" wars of the past. Unless we can see even the quiet war, the war of subterfuge and subversion and subtle diplomacy, for what it really is—a crusade to eradicate a nation, a society and a culture—and unless we realize that internal Arab conflicts revolve around tactics and not the supreme goal, the conspiracy will continue to grow until the Arabs overwhelm Israel.

It is impossible to envision this without seeing, too, a war in the Middle East so cataclysmic, so brutal and so truly genocidal that there can be only one name for it:

Armageddon.

2

*J*ihad

On October 6, 1975, two years after the Arabs launched the Yom Kippur War, the Middle East News Agency picked up an episode of Anwar el-Sadat's memoirs from *Al Anwar,* the Cairo newspaper, and the Arab world heard Sadat's own version of his emotions when word reached the Egyptian Operations Room that the first air strike against the Israeli positions in the Sinai were under way:

"Then there was unparalleled and magnificent joy. I was sitting very calmly. If anybody had been able to reach my soul in those immortal moments, he would have felt a strange kind of tranquillity spreading all over my body. At the time, I felt none of the worries which had burdened me since the 1967 defeat. As I said before, all the worries disappeared by our breaking the barrier of fear, defeat, degradation, humiliation, loss, division and all symptoms of illness from which our Arab nation and dear Egypt suffered. . . ."

By our standards, that paragraph embodies a terrifying

series of excesses. It relates, in fact, to the reactions of a sane man who has just unloosed an army composed of people just like himself against an enemy which had been vilified for decades in terms beyond our imagining. A whole race, 150 million strong, believed, as Sadat did, that the entire "Arab nation" had been disgraced by the Jews of Israel. And nothing was to be permitted to stand in the way of the reclamation of Arab honor. *Nothing.*

After the Six-Day War, it became fashionable in certain Western circles to say that only the erasure of this terrible and corrosive feeling of degradation could ever balance the scales sufficiently to make peace possible. The Arabs themselves endlessly repeated this refrain like an anthem, and with it they used such words as "mercy" and "generosity" toward the enemy they would one day vanquish. The rest—the genocidal threats, the thirst for blood—was not to be taken seriously.

The Israelis thought differently. It was their men who had been mutilated in previous wars, their prisoners of war who had disappeared into the hell that was called prison in Syria, their children whose schoolyards were being guarded against terrorist attacks.

When the Yom Kippur War erupted, there were horrifying rumors in Israel. The son of a highly placed government official returned home and unexpectedly died; Jerusalemites told each other that he had drunk from a well poisoned by retreating Syrian troops. There were whispers of the murder and mutilation of Israeli POWs. The Israeli government refused to comment.

"Supposing it's true?" one official snapped. "They would all have parents to hear it, wouldn't they? What do you think we are? Arabs?"

Photographs of atrocities committed by Arabs were brought to the United States a few months later. They were shown to some members of Congress, including Bella Abzug. They were also shown to *Newsweek,* which refused to print them in a family magazine.

But the Israeli press printed stories and the rumors continued. Then in November and December of 1973, the Israelis filed complaints with the International Red Cross of forty-two cases of murder of captured soldiers. In one case, a complaint said, a body was found with the hands and feet bound and the eyes gouged out. In another, five captives were bound, beaten with rifle butts until "the cries were plainly heard" outside the room where they were held, and then killed.

"The Government of Israel," said a formal complaint, "has reliable information that a Moroccan soldier serving with the Syrian forces had a sack filled with parts of bodies of Israeli soldiers (palms and tongues) which he intended to send home as souvenirs."

Prisoners, Israel complained, were also displayed to Arab villagers, beaten, knifed and left to die of their wounds.

In a stony *wadi* retaken on the Golan Heights, Israelis found the bodies of eleven of their soldiers, some nude and shoeless, all with their hands bound and their eyes blindfolded. "Examination of the bodies disclosed that the prisoners were shot at very close range."

Was this the whole story? The Israelis thought not. There were still too many missing in action. The Syrians and the Egyptians admitted they still held Israeli prisoners but refused to release lists. Both lists and prisoners had to be paid for in concessions. The Israeli prisoners, when they were finally returned, were very few in number. They told of torture, beatings, sexual attacks and terrible deprivation, but they were not able to account for many of the missing.

Soon after filing their official complaints, the Israelis

found out what had happened to at least some of their men. The testimony came from the lips of the Syrian Defense Minister, Mustafa Tlas, and it was made in the Syrian National Assembly. It can be found in the December, 1973, minutes of that body. Tlas was speaking of the "supreme valor" of a Syrian soldier:

"There is the outstanding case of a recruit from Aleppo who murdered twenty-eight Jewish soldiers all by himself, slaughtering them like sheep. All of his comrades witnessed this. He butchered three of them with an ax and decapitated them. In other words, instead of using a gun to kill them, he took a hatchet to chop their heads off. He struggled face to face with one of them and, throwing down his ax, managed to break his neck and devour his flesh in front of his companions."

Tlas went on to assure his listeners in the legislature that "this is a special case." Rhetorically, he asked: "Need I single him out to award him the Medal of the Republic? I will grant this medal to any soldier who succeeds in killing twenty-eight Jews, and I will cover him with appreciation and honor his bravery."

Three generations of Arabs have been raised on horrors such as this. They have been raised to terrorize and murder. The people chosen to do the killing are the ill-educated and often primitive conscripts of the Arab world. But the responsibility rests with educated men, even with religious leaders. It is their doing that an illiterate Syrian conscript not only murders but is deified for his atrocity.

"I shall see the hatred in the eyes of my son and your sons," wrote Nasr Al-Din an-Nashashibi, scion of a distinguished Palestinian family, in 1962. "I shall see how they take revenge. If they do not know how to take revenge, I shall teach them. And if they agree to a truce or peace, I shall fight against them as I fight against my enemy and theirs. I want them to be callous, to be ruthless, to take revenge. I want them to wash away the disaster of 1948 [when invading Arab armies failed to overwhelm the new-born State of Israel] with the blood of those who prevent them from entering their land. Their homeland is dear to them, but revenge is dearer. We'll enter their lairs in Tel Aviv. We'll smash Tel Aviv with axes, guns, hands, fingernails and teeth. . . ."

Nashashibi's son must now be grown. If he has survived the holocaust in Lebanon, he has only one enemy left. Yet, he can know very little about Israel or the Israelis. Since his father's dreadful jeremiad, there have been two wars. A monstrous obsession gripped the entire Arab world after the earlier of those wars, which in six days of fighting resulted in great slices of territory lost to men they considered an inferior race. The 1973 attack was to become almost a physical necessity to the Arabs. It is against this background that the sick savagery of the Yom Kippur War was played out. The struggle had become *jihad*, a holy duty.

Between the two wars, in 1971, the Egyptian Government Printing Office published the minutes of a religious summit conference held to discuss Israel. The conference itself had taken place in 1968, but the issues were still very much alive. The Fourth Conference of the Academy of Islamic Research was held at the prestigious Al Azhar University in Cairo. It was attended by the Mufti of Lebanon and by Islamic leaders from ten countries. All the clergymen present were state officials—there are no secular states in the Arab world, Islam is the state religion everywhere (except in agonized Lebanon) and every cleric is supported by the government. The purpose of the conference was to back the struggle against Israel. Its minutes filled three volumes. Its format was in keeping with the scholarship of its participants: the gathering heard papers, read by their authors.

"I have thoroughly scrutinized the nature of the Jews," said one Islamic savant. "They are avaricious, ruthless, cruel, hypocritical and revengeful. These traits govern their lives. They never change. . . . They always try to seize an opportunity to take revenge on Islam and Moslems."

"The Jews of Mohammed's time," said another scholarly clergyman, "rightfully deserved the wrath and the curse of Allah" because they had committed "unlawful and forbidden crimes" and "sowed the seeds of suspicion and doubt among the people. . . . It has been prescribed for them to be thus dispersed upon the earth."

It was therefore impossible for Moslems to treat with Jews for peace, a third paper pointed out, "since it has been proven beyond doubt that they are a mere gang of robbers and criminals to whom trust, faith and conscience mean nothing."

The Mufti of Tarsus in Syria told the gathering that Jews within the community have always been "a curse that spreads among the people, bringing about corruption, sowing the seeds of enmity and hatred and breaking the bonds of brotherhood."

The "wicked behavior" of the Jews was attributed by one sage to the fact that "their Holy Book taught them the worst that a teacher could teach his pupils." Jews were referred to, with the Koran cited as the source, as "an enemy which is devoid of any human feeling . . . a pest and a plague that is cursed like Satan."

The conference concluded that it was necessary to continue the struggle. The Islamic spiritual leaders adopted a resolution declaring *jihad*—sanctified war—on "Israeli aggression." As the Mufti of Lebanon explained, "when the enemies occupy an Islamic area . . . *jihad* then becomes an enjoinment in person" and it becomes the duty of "every able person of the Muslims" to "fight by all means to rescue his country" and to defend his honor. The learned Mufti continued:

"To those who are far away, *jihad* is an enjoinment by proxy, namely it can be executed or adopted . . . on behalf of others who are not obliged to take part in [the] fighting.

"The ways of supporting and consolidating the fighters of *jihad,* such as providing them with money, employing their tongues and pens, resorting to political tactics and urging the people to share in that fighting, are indeed part and parcel of the *jihad* as an enjoinment in person."

Obviously, according to the Mufti's interpretation, an oil emir a thousand miles from the battle zone who funded anti-Israel terrorists, bought tanks for a front-line army, paid for PLO propaganda or bribed delgates to the UN was participating in noble *jihad* even as was the bomb-hurling killer or the raiding soldier.

The Mufti went on to emphasize and elaborate. ". . . The *jihad* in the cause of Allah—namely, fighting in the different sectors of Palestine—is an enjoinment in person" upon every trained Moslem of Palestine and every Moslem citizen in Egypt, Jordan and Syria. "It is thus an enjoinment by proxy upon all other Moslems who are far away from those areas and places. . . ."

With approval, the Mufti pointed to the views of scholars who believed that "the Moslems who are distant from the battlefield of Palestine, such as the Algerians, the Moroccans, all the Africans, Saudi Arabian people, Yemeni people, the Indians, Iraqi people, the Russians and the Europeans are indeed sinful if they do not hasten to offer all possible means to achieve success and gain victory in the Islamic battle between two religions (namely, it is a religious battle). Zionism in fact represents a very perilous cancer, aiming at domineering [*sic*] the Arab countries and the whole Islamic world."

The enjoinment of *jihad* was not just an idle statement to be filed away and forgotten. Years later, if Anwar el-Sadat felt "a strange kind of tranquillity spreading all over my body" when word reached him of the attack on Israeli positions on the Suez, the soldiers manning those positions felt something else. Israeli reservists, looking into the eyes of the Egyptian troops who burst with unbelievable ferocity into their bunkers, thought they were drugged. What they saw was the psychedelic fury of *jihad.*

Every Egyptian soldier who went into battle that day carried a pocket-sized leaflet entitled "Our Faith—Our Way to Victory," published in an edition of one million copies by the Egyptian Army. It consisted of excerpts from the Koran, Islam's holy work, with an introduction by the Chief of the General Staff, Lt. Gen. Sa'ad Shazli:

My sons, officers and men—Sons of Egypt, best soldiers on earth, scions of the great Pharaohs, sons of the intrepid Arabs! The time has come to purge our souls of the degradation and humiliation that we suffered after the defeat of 1967. . . .

My sons, officers and men—The Jews have overstepped the bounds in injustice and deceit. And we sons of Egypt have determined to set them back on their heels . . . killing and destroying so as to wash away the shame of th defeat and to restore our honor and pride. Kill them w. er you find them (see Koran 2.191, 4.91) and take heed t they do not deceive you, for they are a treacherous peopl They may feign surrender in order to gain power over you and kill you vilely.

Kill them and let not compassion or mercy for them seize you! . . . Avenge yourselves and the souls of the sons of

Egypt! We must enter the battle with the motto, "Victory or martyrdom." If this is our motto, victory is at our heels, by Allah's grace.

Moslem authorities in Egypt, Syria and Saudi Arabia duly and officially declared the October, 1973, war as *jihad.* Nearly two years later, Hassan Touhamy, Secretary General of the Islamic Conference of Foreign Ministers, spoke of one of the aims of a forthcoming meeting of those powerful men: "The Conference will discuss the formation of Islamic 'struggle and *jihad*' brigades to liberate Jerusalem and occupied Palestine."

The Arab world's deep and abiding hatred of Jews goes back more than a millennium before the evolution of modern political Zionism. The prophet of Allah, Mohammed himself, said: "Certainly you will find that the biggest enemies of the Believers are the Jews and the polytheists." Jew-hatred needed no state called Israel and it had no need to characterize Jews as Semites. To this day, Arabs are notably uninterested in any possible common heritage with Jews. Insulting, Nazi-like cartoons of dwarfed, greasy, hook-nosed Jews frequently appear in the Arab press. It has apparently never occurred to the Arab editors who print this garbage that it might be interpreted as referring to the wrong kind of Semites. To this failure in cognition can be added a malignant bigotry.

Col. Muammar el-Qaddafi of Libya keeps on his desk a stack of the *Protocols of the Elders of Zion* for distribution to visitors. The tract is a notorious fraud, a primitive turn-of-the-century Tsarist Russian libel purporting to be a documented account of a Jewish plot to conquer the world. "It is a most important historic document," Qaddafi assured a Western journalist.

33

In giving a copy to an Indian editor, Gamal Abdel Nasser of Egypt expressed the opinion that the pamphlet proved "beyond a shadow of a doubt that three hundred Zionists, each of whom knows all the others, govern the fate of the European continent." Nasser's brother published one of the many editions of the *Protocols* which have been circulated throughout the Arab world.

The late King Feisal of Saudi Arabia offered to give a copy of the *Protocols* to Henry Kissinger, who had already sat through a lengthy orientation briefing on why the Jews created Communism (to subdue the world). Earlier, in August, 1972, Feisal had given an interview to a Lebanese reporter in which he said of the making of matzoth, the unleavened bread of Passover:

"It happened that two years ago, while I was in Paris on a visit, the police discovered five murdered children. Their blood had been drained, and it turned out that some Jews had murdered them in order to take their blood and mix it with the bread that they eat on this day. This shows you what is the extent of their hatred and malice toward non-Jewish peoples."

At that time, the *Protocols of the Elders of Zion* was a best-seller in Beirut. In Kuwait, the tract was translated into English, Spanish and French for export. Jordan's Premier Wasfi Tal, who disliked terrorists and was later assassinated by Yasir Arafat's Black September terror squad, quoted the *Protocols* in a university lecture as supporting evidence of the "world-wide Jewish conspiracy."

The *Protocols* form, by now, part and parcel of the oral tradition of the Arab world and are referred to time and again as accepted fact. Anti-Semitism is included in army indoctrination and taught in grade schools. For the past quarter-century and more, Arab schoolchildren have been using inflammatory school texts. A few samples:

"The Jews in Europe were persecuted and despised because of their corruption, meanness and treachery." (Jordanian reader.)

"We can never forget how the Jews tormented Mohammed, the prophet of Allah." (Egyptian reader for third graders.)

"By their nature, they are vile, greedy and enemies of mankind." (Syrian junior high school reader.)

"The Jews are the enemies of the Arabs. Soon we will rescue Palestine from their hands." (Writing exercise for Syrian first graders.)

"Analyze: 'We shall expel all the Jews from the Arab countries.'" (Exercise in "basic syntax" for Syrian fifth graders.)

> "You Jews shall never have a homeland—
> You never had a homeland—
> We will take over Palestine—
> And bury you in its soil."
>
> (Egyptian writing text for junior high schools.)

In 1968, René Maheu, director general of UNESCO, the UN body devoted to education and culture, made inquiries of the Syrian Minister of Education about the content of his schoolbooks. The answer was prompt: "The hatred which we indoctrinate into the minds of our children from their birth is sacred."

Given the pervasive anti-Jewish heritage of Islam, it is not surprising that key Arab figures in the twentieth century have found it easy to ally themselves with Hitler and Nazism. They ranged from the notorious Grand Mufti of Jerusalem, Haj Amin el Husseini, who fled to Berlin at the height of World War II and praised Nazi methods for dealing with the Jews, to the respectable Anwar el-Sadat of Egypt, a zealous anti-Semite all his adult life.

The official record on Sadat begins during World War II

when Rommel was sweeping toward Alexandria. It was 1941 and a hard and discouraging time for the Allies. The untried Egyptian army, equipped and trained by the British, was sorely needed, but it was unreliable and its chief of staff, Aziz el Masri, had been forced out by the British as pro-Nazi. "FILE SOONEST THOUSAND WORDS WILL EGYPTIANS FIGHT," a British newspaper cabled its Cairo correspondent. His reply was to become a classic in journalistic annals: "NO NO THOUSAND TIMES NO." And where, at this point, was Sadat? Gamal Abdel Nasser, Sadat's predecessor as Egypt's president, was to describe Sadat's efforts to smuggle Gen. el Masri, the deposed chief of staff, through the British lines to the German army. In a ludicrous series of jeep breakdowns and plane crashes, the attempt failed. Nasser, confiding to an interviewer later that "our sympathy was with the Nazis," heard the bad news in the desert outpost where he himself was marooned beyond plotting. "But for bad luck," Sadat wrote Nasser, "we would have joined forces with the Axis, struck a quick blow at the British and helped win the war. Better luck next time." Next time Sadat made contact with German headquarters in Libya, his objective the setting up of a German spy unit. He was found out and spent two years in a British jail.

His views did not change over the years. In 1953, when Sadat was one of the tight little coterie of officers around Nasser, a rumor swept Egypt that Hitler was still alive. Sadat, along with other leading Egyptians, was asked by an enterprising Cairo weekly what he might write to the Führer if indeed the rumor was true.

"Dear Hitler," Sadat wrote in a message published in the September 18, 1953, issue of *Al Musawwar,* "I congratulate you from the bottom of my heart. Even if you appear to be defeated, in reality you are the victor. . . . You may be proud of having become the immortal leader of Germany.

We will not be surprised if you appear again in Germany or if a new Hitler rises up in your wake.''

Two years later, Sadat, then a Minister of State, spread the clear message of *jihad* courtesy of Cairo radio: "Our war against the Jews is an old battle which Mohammed began. . . . It is our duty to fight the Jews in the name of Allah and in the name of our religion, and it is our duty to finish the war which Mohammed began.''

Even the mantle of the presidency did not transform Sadat. Late in 1975, during a visit to the United States whose main purpose was to demonstrate his moderation, Sadat told Washington newsmen in all seriousness that the Jews "had our economy in their hands'' until the 1950s. Back home—in Arabic—he was more to the point. On April 25, 1972, the day of the anniversary of Mohammed's death, he broadcast yet another message over Cairo radio:

"We shall not only liberate the Arab lands in Jerusalem and break Israel's pride in victory, but we will return them to the state in which the Koran described them before: to be persecuted, suppressed and miserable!''

The Arab hatred of Jews is an ancient one. The periods when Jews lived among the Arabs as respected equals were few and of short duration. Even the "golden age" of Moslem Spain was only a luminous interlude in a long twilight. Maimonides, the great twelfth-century Jewish philosopher most often cited by Arab apologists as an example of the tolerance of this era, is equally a symbol of its fragility. Maimonides fled Spain when his protectors were deposed by a more fanatical branch of Islam.

Since the lifetime of Mohammed, the Jews in Arab lands have been persecuted because of their refusal to accept Islam. Officially classified as *dhimmi,* a minority community "protected" because of its monotheism, they were forced to wear distinctive garments identifying them as Jews, they were taxed as Jews, they were barred from carrying weapons in a society where arms were both insurance and symbols of manly dignity. In some jurisdictions they were forbidden to sit in the presence of a Moslem or to pass a Believer on the right. "Protection" often gave way to forcible conversion and, for the obdurate, death.

The Russians have provided posterity with the term, but they did not invent the pogrom. There have been pogroms in Arab countries for thirteen centuries, pogroms based upon the insidious libel of ritual murder by Jews to obtain blood for Passover matzoth, and ending with cries for vengeance that resulted in rapine and the death of countless innocent persons.

The Koran itself, a gospel powerfully alive among a people still firm and unquestioning in their faith, celebrates Mohammed's wrath against the Jews of Beni Quaraidha and his orders for the draconian punishment of this intractably Mosaic tribe. All of its males, seven hundred of them, were put to death. John Bagot Glubb, known as Glubb Pasha, former commander of Jordan's impressive Arab Legion, wrote of this seventh-century execution in terms reminiscent of Babi Yar and other scenes of Nazi atrocity: "Trenches were dug during the night near the main market of Medina," this Arabist wrote in his *Life and Times of Muhammad.* "In the morning, the Jews were led in small batches, their hands tied behind their backs, and made to kneel down beside the trench. Before execution they were offered conversion to Islam, but few took advantage of the offer."

Pogroms swept North Africa frequently in medieval times. In 1790, the Sultan of Morocco launched a bloodletting of terrible ferocity against the Jews. Ghettoization came soon after, with Jews forced into barred *mellahs*

38

across North Africa. As late as 1890 Algeria witnessed a wave of bloody attacks on Jews.

Fifteen years later a U.S. consul attested that Jews in Tangiers, "falsely accused of the most fearful crimes, had been barbarously tortured and many executed." The Jews, wrote U.S. Secretary of State Elihu Root, were subject to "painful and injurious restrictions," their situation "well-nigh incredible."

In 1941, Iraqi mobs slaughtered 185 Baghdad Jews and left two thousand injured to crawl out of their wrecked and looted homes. Four years later, during the period Arabs describe as one of "peaceful coexistence" in Egypt, mobs raced through the streets of Cairo and Alexandria, pillaging, burning synagogues and killing.

The rioting spread rapidly to neighboring Libya. From Tripoli, its capital, a New York *Times* correspondent wrote: "Babies were beaten to death with iron bars. Old men were hacked to pieces where they fell. Expectant mothers were disemboweled. Whole families were burned alive in their homes. When the riots were raging, the thirst for blood seemed to have supplanted the desire for loot and vengeance."

That sort of genocidal image is very far from the image the Arabs seek to project today, when new initiatives to the West have become important. But hatred of Jews is too deeply ingrained in the area to be suppressed. It is freely preached in the mosques and it appears, time and again, in official publications. Thus, Egypt's Military Research Organization, an arm of government, distributed a leaflet at an international symposium on the "consequences" of the Yom Kippur War, held in Cairo in 1975, which said, in part: "No country admits Jews in its armed forces, because every country knows very well that they are no combatants

THE PLOT TO DESTROY ISRAEL

. . . they have concentrated their efforts in dominating the resources of wealth. They dominated the banks, insurance companies, the markets and information media. . . . Their weapons are cheating, deceit, and exploitation of other people's misfortunes, because their only loyalty is to money and not to the country in which they live." The Military Research Organization's contribution to the symposium was intended as an anti-Israel statement, making no differentiation between Jews and Israelis or Jews and Zionists.

Deceit and cheating, of course, are matters of definition. The Palestine Liberation Organization advocated an interesting policy in a pamphlet distributed among the faithful: "The goal is to put an end to the Zionist character of the promised land, but we must not define our goal in this way, so that no person will be able to accuse us of fascism or of anti-Semitism, because we are dependent to a great extent on world opinion."

It was a clever line, but perhaps too subtle for perfect implementation. Contradictions kept cropping up. In July, 1976, Yasir Arafat, taking a moment off from the war of Christian and Moslem in Lebanon, sent a message urging that "the international seminar on Zionism and racism," held in all solemnity in Libya, "emphasize that Jews have nothing to do with Zionism . . . and are victims of Zionism." That same month the Voice of Palestine proudly announced that explosives planted by "our Palestinian fighters" had destroyed "a Zionist bus" near Tel Aviv and killed or injured "several Zionists." The Voice of Palestine, Arafat's radio, did not explain how it knew that the hapless bus riders were Zionists, not simply Jews.

Double Exposure

Like the goals of the Palestinian terrorists, the goals of the Arab states are unchanged; it is the manner of their presentation to the outside world that has changed, particularly since the 1973 war. Not even President Hafez al-Assad of Syria was able to ignore the new importance of presenting an image of moderation to the critical eyes of the Western world. His difficulty lay in reconciling what he said for foreign consumption with what he said at home.

Assad told *Newsweek*'s chief diplomatic correspondent that "the last obstacle to a final settlement" would be removed if Israel were to evacuate the territory occupied since the Six-Day War and permit the establishment of a Palestinian state on that territory. There would then be "a formal peace treaty. . . . We are not looking for a limited agreement—but a lasting peace." Further, he said, this did not represent "a new logic on Syria's part."

It was, in fact, important news, reflecting the first swing toward formal peace by an Arab leader. In March, 1975,

41

Newsweek ran the full text of the interview in question-and-answer form. The denial from Damascus was immediate and came straight from Assad's own office. *Newsweek*'s published interview, said a formal statement, did not "correctly reflect its content, especially the question of a peace agreement." Damascus radio and the Arab media instantly echoed the disclaimer and Assad himself went before a group of Syrian students the next day with a different message:

"Peace is not determined by Damascus or Cairo, it is determined by the Palestinian people. . . . I wish the rights of the Palestinian people in their entirety. . . . Our struggle is based on the view that the Arab land is one entity. We are struggling for the liberation of the collective entity."

In the West, the Syrian denial went almost unmarked. In the Arab world, the *Newsweek* interview was buried under denial while Assad's call for the "liberation of the collective entity" was recognized for what it actually was: the "collective entity" includes the entire State of Israel.

The Arabs have learned to use the Western press as a vehicle for statements of "moderation" which are then denied at home. This yields a double dividend: abroad, the statements of peaceful intent are likely to be front-of-the-paper news and the denials no news at all; at home, where foreign publications are read only by sophisticates, the denials in the local media dominate, serving to reinforce the claim that "Zionist imperialists" are spreading lies to weaken the resolve to destroy Israel.

On April 5, 1974, a PLO representative, Said Hammami, chose the *London Jewish Chronicle* as a vehicle. He told the weekly newspaper that the PLO had been misquoted as saying that its aims were the liberation of all of Palestine.

"We recognize that a new Israeli people has been created," he said. "The creation of the Palestine Arab State would draw out the poison. . . . We would, in fact, propose open boundaries with Israel."

Hammami went on to state that Yasir Arafat was ready to meet with Golda Meir face-to-face, reiterating: "Yes, why not? What are the Geneva peace talks if not face-to-face?"

That night the Beirut newspaper *An-Nahar* carried an official PLO statement which denied every point made in the interview:

"We have no knowledge of these things. They do not express the view of the organization. The strategic aim of the PLO is the establishment of a democratic state in the whole land of Palestine, in which everybody—Christians, Moslems and Jews—will coexist without racialism, discrimination, fanaticism or fascism."

In past decades, the war of words was carried on without such dichotomies for local and foreign consumption. Kings and presidents spoke fearlessly, and without regard for public relations tactics; they said exactly what they believed.

Gamal Abdel Nasser, who dominated the Arab scene for nearly twenty years, said in 1969: "The Arab nation has decided to embark on the path of war. . . . We will move on to the containment of Israel and after that to its eradication."

President Houari Boumédiene of Algeria declared that same year: "The true freedom of the entire homeland must be won through the liquidation of the Zionist state."

Jordan's King Hussein said after the 1967 war: "Israel makes no sense, geographically or economically."

In 1964, the Syrian army Chief of Staff said: "Our army will accept nothing short of the disappearance of Israel."

The Foreign Minister of Iraq said in 1960: "Israel has no right whatsoever to continue to exist in the territories of the Arab East."

In 1967, Nasser said: "Our basic objective will be the destruction of Israel." In 1955, he told an American journalist: "The hatred of the Arabs is very strong and there is no sense in talking of peace with Israel."

That same year, Syria's Premier said: "The Arabs will not rest as long as this thieving enemy still dwells on holy soil in the very heart of the Arab world."

King Feisal of Saudi Arabia said in 1969: "There will be strains in the Middle East until the State of Israel is removed."

Such statements were rarely to be found in Western newspapers in the mid-1970s. Their absence was no accident but a matter of policy, the result of growing sophistication and growing understanding of the semi-science of communications. Why rouse sleeping liberals when you can win hearts and minds and disguise goals with soft words? In one case—that of Egypt—the tactic matched the immediate needs of diplomacy. In the 1975 disengagement accord brokered by Henry Kissinger, Egypt won its principal demand: Israeli withdrawal from the Sinai oil fields and from a pair of strategic passes. One of the few Egyptian gestures in return was a pledge to soften the tone of the fulminations which had been aimed at Israel for decades. This pleased the State Department which, naturally, had found the flood of filth broadcast by Egypt an embarrassing contradiction to the line of peace via step-by-step diplomacy.

It was Egypt's Sadat, more than any other single individual, who evolved for the West the new public-relations package of Arab moderation. "We shall continue the struggle with honor and the help of Allah," he told Egypt's National Council on June 23, 1973, "until the day when all the

Arab homeland is purged of the Zionist crime and its consequences." Half a year later he cast himself in a different
role. It was a mere fourteen days after the Yom Kippur
guns fell silent when Sadat graciously received the American Secretary of State and then graciously joined Kissinger
in an appearance before the international media. "I think,"
Dr. Kissinger concluded after only three hours of talks,
"we are moving toward peace." Sadat smiled at his new
friend and said: "I agree with him. For me, let it be immediately."

The State Department found it convenient to embrace
the new Sadat and ignore the old, but there was no persua-
sive evidence of transformation. With Sadat, the pitch was
always attuned to the audience. Among trustworthy friends
he remained the man of war, for the West he was a man of
peace. In the mid-summer of 1976, nearly three years after
he first hugged and kissed Dr. Kissinger and spoke solemnly of peace, Sadat made these contrasting statements in a
matter of weeks:

To the Egyptian public, in a live broadcast: ". . . the
glorious October [1973] War . . . shook the earth under
the feet of Israel and cracked Israel's psychological
edifice."

To the American vice-president of the Reader's Digest
Foundation: If Israel were to retreat, a Palestinian mini-
state were established and "the Palestine problem
. . . solved," Egypt "will end the state of war . . . [and]
then try to build lasting peace in the entire region."

To his old allies at the fifth Non-Aligned Conference at
Sri Lanka (in a speech unnoticed by the Western media):
Egypt had taught Israel a "lesson" in October, 1973, but Israel remained a "source of aggression" and needed a new
"lesson" to dispel "illusions of superiority and domina-
tion."

45

To the Arab world: "Our brothers in the occupied territories [must] . . . continue their struggle and heroic resistance against the tyrannical Israeli occupation."

All things are comparative. Sadat needed infusions of American money and so he *did* lower the decibel level of Cairo's propaganda. That lasted about a year and then the many voices of Cairo began to grow shrill again.

The Arab campaign of cruel and militant words is waged across the Middle East—in Arabic and often, in reflection of sympathies and political passions, in the vocabulary of "revolution." Loaded with fury against Israel, these tirades form an obsessive litany in news stories, radio broadcasts, TV dramas and commentaries, editorials, poems and novels. These are for *Arab* consumption but they are monitored—among many others—by the U.S. government. The following, taken from the daily bulletins of the federal Foreign Broadcast Information Service (FBIS), are typical of the cascade of *Arabic* statements *after* the advances of step-by-step diplomacy:

"The essence of our struggle [revolves around] the expulsion of the Palestinian Arab people from their homeland by Israel, which since 1948 has been carrying out an aggressive policy . . . in its capacity as the spearhead of aggression brandished against the Arab nation." (Damascus radio.)

"Sudan's strategy on the Arab question is in three stages: withdrawal from the territory Israel occupied in 1967, withdrawal from the 1947 territory, and the Palestinians' determination of the question as they see fit." (President Jaafir el-Nemery of the Sudan in an interview with an Arabic newspaper.)

Saudi Arabia is preparing for all eventualities, "whether for peace based on right and justice, or for a defensive or

liberation war to retrieve all the occupied Arab territories
and regain the usurped rights from the Zionist enemy."
(King Khalid of Saudi Arabia.)

"The first stage of the struggle for national liberation
must be the overthrow and destruction of the basic struc-
tures of the racist Zionist entity by political and military
means." (Nayif Hawatmeh, leader of the Democratic Popular Front for the Liberation of Palestine, to a Kuwaiti
newspaper.)

"The Zionist existence in our homeland is one of the er-
rors which human history is witness to. This error cannot
continue. . . . The necessity of the demise of this error
obligates the Arab nation to mount its preparations and
concentrations to achieve the final victory and to restore
history in our homeland to its natural state." (*Al Ba'ath,*
the newspaper of Syria's ruling party.)

"Zionism is the ugliest form of racialism and colonialism
and, represented in its entity in Palestine, continues in its
sins, obduracy and flouting of all principles of peace and
justice." (King Khalid, in a speech read for him at the Sixth
Conference of Islamic Foreign Ministers in Jiddah, Saudi
Arabia.)

The statements quoted above are not rarities but part of
the daily verbal diet fed to the Arabs. The text on the following pages is culled from FBIS transcripts for a single
day of monitoring of the Arab domestic media. The date—
December 9, 1975—was chosen at random. It could have
been any day—in essence, they are all the same. In the file
for this particular day, one of the first items was a speech
by President Ahmed Hassan al-Bakr of Iraq broadcast over
Baghdad radio, Iraqi television, "the Voice of the Masses"
and Kurdish radio and, presumably, heard by millions:

47

In the name of God the merciful and the compassionate. Great people, masses of the great Arab nation. . . . The imperialist and world Zionist forces and local agent groups have sought for scores of years to undermine our nation, paralyze its will and usurp its rights. These forces have used terrorism in all its forms, maneuvers, misleadings, the spreading of despair . . . and all the arts at their command. . . .

The plot . . . was aimed not only at us in Iraq, but was a link in a large imperialist-Zionist chain of plots to circumvent freedom and revolution and to create atmospheres of defeatism and capitulation . . . in preparation for imposing capitulationist solutions on the Arab nation and . . . [assuring] the survival of the fascist expansionist Zionist entity. . . .

When the glorious October, 1973 battles broke out, the revolution in Iraq kindled the spark of the battles by using oil in the battle. . . . We profoundly believe in the ability of the Arab masses . . . to struggle against the Zionist enemy. . . .

U.S. imperialism, world Zionism and all quarters . . . hostile to the Arabs are trying . . . to preoccupy the Arab nation with conflicts and secondary contradictions . . . in an effort to retain occupation and impose humiliating conditions. . . .

We are called upon to strongly confront this broad Zionist imperialist conspiracy. . . . The Palestine issue was and still is the Arabs' first cause. . . . We . . . affirm that the program of long-term struggle based on the rejection of capitulationist solutions and settlement is the sound and practical program. . . .

Glory to our people and nation. Victory to them in their just struggle. Peace be upon you.

In the jargon of the war against Israel, a "capitulationist solution" means agreement with Israel because any agreement, no matter how minor, involves *de facto* recognition of Israel's right to exist. Iraq committed forces to the wars of 1948, 1967 and 1973 but never signed a cease-fire with Israel.

Iraq's President al-Bakr was still speaking on Iraqi radio and TV when the Voice of Palestine beamed this item to the Arab world:

"The head of the PLO Political Department, Brother Abu Lutf, has said that the recent Israeli attacks on the Palestinian camps is [*sic*] a clear indication that Zionism is synonymous with racism. . . . He added that his current visit to Italy came during an important phase in which all the peoples of the world agree on the need to establish an independent Palestinian state."

Three hours later the Voice of Palestine made clear that the borders of the "independent state" would encompass present-day Israel: "At an early hour today the Palestinian fighters . . . of the groups operating inside the occupied homeland" blew up a number of "enemy vehicles" in an Israeli township in the Galilee.

A columnist in *Ar-Ra'y,* a Jordanian newspaper, complained that Britain and several other nations had voted improperly at the UN on the question of seating the PLO. "Such being the case," the columnist asked rhetorically, "wherein lies the weight of the 'surplus' Arab billions in London? . . . And what is the usefulness of the huge investments the Arab countries are negotiating with Japan? . . . We do not call for the carrying of wooden swords in international dealings, but we urge that these swords be shaken in the face in order at least to halt this state of hypocrisy."

From Tripoli, capital of Libya, came words that a visiting "Palestinian trade union delegation" and Libyan unionists had signed a joint communiqué condemning "American-

Israeli plots against the Palestinians" and announcing "absolute rejection of any form of colonial existence and imperialistic influence in the Arab homeland."

Baghdad radio, on its domestic service, carried a statement by 'Abd al-'Aziz al-Wajih, member of the PLO executive committee, praising the Iraqi regime for a recent decision "granting Jews who left Iraq after 1948 the right to return." (Most of those Iraqi Jews were citizens of Israel and were subject, according to PLO official resolutions, to expulsion once the PLO state was formed.) This "historic decision," he said, ". . . constitutes a hallmark on the road to complete liberation and uprooting of the Zionist society as a prelude to the achievement of our comprehensive nationalist aims."

"We are nearer," the PLO man said in summarizing his visit, "to achieving our nationalist aims of liberating all our occupied land through elimination of the usurper Zionist entity which imperialism planted in the heart of our Arab homeland to prevent the progress of our nation. . . ."

Anwar el-Sadat of Egypt granted an interview and the newsman quoted him to the effect that "it was illogical and unjust to ask the Palestinians, after stripping them of their rights and land for twenty-seven years, to recognize Israel. He added that, if he were a Palestinian, he would certainly not do so."

Sadat was also quoted thus: "We have not put an end to the state of war by the second disengagement agreement. Everybody knows that we have only decided not to use force during the duration of the agreement." The agreement, signed in September, 1975, was renewable annually for three years.

Damascus radio reported that, during a visit, East German Foreign Minister Oskar Fischer said his country supported "firmly the just struggle of the Arab nation against the imperialist Israeli aggression."

Sudan's Omdurman radio announced that India's President Fakhurddin Ali Ahmed, in a meeting with Sudan's President Nemery, had "stressed in particular the regaining by the Palestinian people of their land. . . . In brief, His Excellency . . . was hinting that we should not lose the Spirit of October."

Damascus radio reported that President Hafez al-Assad met with Libyan Prime Minister Abdel Salam Jalloud to discuss "the pooling of Arab forces and resources required by the current phase to confront the imperialist and Zionist plots. . . ."

Revolutionary Libya and conservative Kuwait, in a joint statement marking the Kuwaiti foreign minister's visit to Tripoli, affirmed "unlimited support . . . for the Palestinian Arab people until their goal of completely liberating Palestine is achieved."

For the great Arab public, in short, Dec. 9, 1975, was a day like any other day. The daily diet of hate was broadcast and absorbed, the anti-Israel and anti-Jewish passions and hatreds were reinforced. The day's statements were clear enough; only one point of fact, perhaps, needed to be added for a Western reader: Except for Beirut, there were no privately owned or controlled news organs in the Arab world. The statements quoted above were disseminated by state-owned or -policed outlets. These statements—though Western media found them lacking in news value, though Western governments found it convenient to ignore them, though the Arabs themselves found it politic to voice other ideas in Washington and London—represented the official views of Arab governments and the sentiments which Arab leaders clearly wanted their people to share.

4

Tactics and Goals

In May, 1967, a furor against Israel swept the Arab world. The Jewish state had been in existence for nineteen years; that was long enough. Great armies, dwarfing the Israeli forces, massed on the borders. And no secret was made of the goal.

Cairo radio announced: "All Egypt is now prepared to plunge into total war which will put an end to Israel."

The next day the Voice of the Arabs said: "The sole method we shall apply against Israel is a total war which will result in the extermination of the Zionist existence."

Three days after that proclamation Hafez al-Assad, then Syria's defense minister and later president, said: "Our forces are now entirely ready . . . to initiate the act of liberation itself and to explode the Zionist presence in the Arab homeland."

Seven days later Gamal Abdel Nasser of Egypt said: "We will not accept . . . any coexistence with Israel."

Western diplomats rushed aimlessly to and fro. The world stood paralyzed. The Arab H-hour approached.

In June, 1967, the Israelis, fearing for their national life, staged a pre-emptive strike against the vastly superior and encircling Arab armies. In six days, Israeli units swept across the Sinai to the Suez, stopped the shelling of Jerusalem by Jordan, drove hard-fighting Jordanian troops to the Jordan River and battled their way up the Golan Heights of Syria. Two weeks later Gen. Moshe Dayan, then Israel's Defense Minister, announced with confidence that he was awaiting a phone call from Cairo or Amman.

His logic was obvious: Israel had decimated three Arab armies and three Arab air forces, and Israel's Arab neighbors lay defenseless before it. The Suez was closed, a million people and a number of Arab cities were in Israeli hands. Yet Israel was ready to give almost all of the conquests back in exchange for peace. Those Arab words of hate, it was believed, had poured out in moments of unthinking passion and would be forgotten during realistic negotiations involving land for peace. Clearly, the Jews and the Arabs were about to meet.

Instead it was the *Arabs* who met, at a watershed summit conference in Khartoum. There the Arab leaders formulated the three Khartoum NO's—NO peace with Israel, NO negotiations with Israel, NO recognition of Israel.

Today, after another, costlier war, after bloody terror, after endless diplomatic maneuvering, Israel still holds most of the territory occupied in 1967—and the Khartoum NO's still apply.

Late in 1970 General Dayan, seeking to build upon a new Suez cease-fire, floated a proposal for an interim settlement involving an Israeli pullback followed by the opening of the canal to commerce. This led to months of complicated and indirect contacts, with American diplomats carrying ideas back and forth, but the attempt failed because Egypt insisted upon a prior Israeli commitment to a staged but—eventually—total withdrawal from the Sinai, without any reciprocal Egyptian pledges leading to peace and mutual acceptance. After the Yom Kippur War, with its thousands of Egyptian dead and its vast Egyptian expenditures, Cairo had obtained little more than that aborted interim settlement of 1970-71 would have provided.

Soon after the 1948 war, Azzam Pasha, the first Secretary-General of the Arab League, a man of stature, culture and influence, said: "We have a secret weapon which we can use better than guns and machine guns, and this is time. As long as we do not make peace with the Zionists, the war is not over. And as long as the war is not over, there is neither victor nor vanquished. As soon as we recognize the existence of the State of Israel, we admit by this act that we are vanquished."

Three wars later, nothing had changed. The Arab world continued to refuse to recognize Israel's right to exist. Israelis were hardly human; for meaningful contact there had to be middle-men. Some Arab states and statesmen refused even to grant Israel the legitimacy of a name and spoke instead of "the Zionist entity." Israel remained a pariah.

After the 1973 Yom Kippur War Henry Kissinger embarked on a mission of shuttle diplomacy unparalleled in diplomatic history. He traveled tens of thousands of air miles, he visited Jerusalem and the Arab capitals repeatedly, he cajoled and promised and threatened and pleaded and blackmailed. He committed the United States to aid and to counsel and, indeed, to station technicians in the Sinai between the combatants. His was a brilliant, exhausting performance.

When it was all over and three "disengagement agreements" had been signed, there was exactly one concrete Arab concession to Israel—Anwar el-Sadat's agreement to permit cargo bound for Israel to pass through the Suez Canal. In legal terms that was something of a travesty because as far back as 1951 the UN Security Council had ruled that Egypt possessed no right to bar Israeli ships from the canal. In practical terms, however, it did represent a concession for in all those years since 1951 Egypt had ignored the UN decision.

No sooner had Sadat kissed Henry Kissinger goodbye than the name of every ship carrying Israel-bound cargo through the Suez appeared, as if by magic, on the blacklist of the Arab Boycott Office.

In 1947 the UN voted, 33 to 13, to establish two states in the territory called Palestine, mandated to Britain after its promise in World War I to aid in building a Jewish National Home in the Holy Land. There were many abstentions to that UN vote. The Arabs had threatened war if the shadow state the Jews had created on reclaimed lands was given recognition. Israel, in fact, was voted into existence only because most of the countries sitting at the UN knew that Hitler had virtually succeeded in wiping out the Jews of Europe simply because there had been no Israel to receive them. The refugee camps were still full of battered, stateless survivors whom no one wanted but the Palestinian Jews. The state was going to be a hard place to live in even without them because it was to be laid out in strict accordance with the existing distribution of the Jewish population—there were 650,000 of them—and their areas of settlement were barely contiguous. On the map, the minuscule

56

new state was shaped more like a question mark with problems than a viable country, and most of it was desert. The Jews said it did not matter. The rest of the country had looked a lot worse before they came and they were confident that they could do something with the Negev desert, too. For them, the hardest problem was Jerusalem, which was to be internationalized. Jews have a feeling for Jerusalem which is akin to a tearing nostalgia. Nevertheless, they were willing to establish a Jewish state without Jerusalem because, under the terms of the UN partition decision, it would be accessible to them. Besides, it was holy to others as well.

Above all, the Jews said, they wanted to have good relations with the Arab state in Palestine and looked forward to a situation comparable to federation, with the two countries cooperating in the peaceful development of the region. But the Zionists were the only ones in the Middle East ready to accept an Arab state in Palestine. The Arabs wanted none of it—because they wanted all of it. Their response was invasion and Azzam Pasha's vow: "This will be a war of extermination and a momentous massacre which will be spoken of like the Mongolian massacres and the Crusades."

Had the Arabs accepted the UN decision, they would today have a state in the greenest and most productive part of Palestine. Its total area would be some five thousand square miles. Three wars later, they were struggling mightily for the establishment of an *interim* Arab state on the West Bank of the Jordan River and in the Gaza Strip. Together, these areas total 2,355 square miles.

Why has it all been necessary? The burning hatred, the refusal to countenance compromise, the readiness to waste life and substance when a little decent flexibility could achieve wonders of peace—these are difficult to fathom. *Ji-*

had is part of the answer, and so is unwavering hatred of the Jew as Jew, but neither seems enough to explain such an extreme attitude, such an unrelenting crusade. Arabs, and those who study their culture, point repeatedly to the code of values of the nomadic bedouin—the archetypical Arab, by now as idealized and totemized as the cowboy in American folklore—and its emphasis on shame and honor. An Arab general, writing shortly after the 1948 war, reported in utter seriousness that the Arabs "regarded the State of Israel as the greatest disaster that has happened to their people. This disaster touched the most vital aspect of their honor and national greatness." Harold W. Glidden, a retired State Department intelligence analyst, in a paper delivered to the American Psychiatric Association in 1972, wrote that in Arab eyes redress of shame could be achieved only by revenge, adding:

"All members of the Arab collectivity are bound to support the cause of their kinsmen, the Palestinian Arabs, who demand the liquidation of Israel as a political entity and the return of the refugee Arabs. This is the vengeance that the Arabs feel must be taken not only to restore to the Palestine Arabs what was wrongfully taken from them, but to eliminate the shame that had been visited upon them and the other Arabs by their defeat in Israel."

But no expert has ever said *when,* in Arab eyes, disgrace is avenged, when shame is wiped out. The Arabs hailed the Yom Kippur War as a great victory, but it did not suffice. The war continues.

The hatred is perpetuated and reinforced by the old Arab habit of endeavoring to avoid the pain of self-criticism by finding others to blame, Israel being the ideal whipping-boy. These attempts usually collapse in time under pressure of events, but they have the cumulative effect of eroding the Arab sense of reality and they result in some remarkable statements. The tragic war of Arab against Arab in Lebanon, as seen by Cairo radio's domestic service in the midst of the killing in September, 1976, represented not an Arab failing but "a major Zionist-imperialist challenge directed at squandering the results" of the 1973 war. Iraq's self-styled "struggle President" al-Bakr, though rarely agreeing with the Egyptians, echoed that thought a few days later, saying that "imperialism and Zionism and their lackeys" were resorting to "physical liquidation" in Lebanon.

To attempt an in-depth psychological analysis of the Arabs is probably a fruitless exercise. The hatred exists. It is a fact of Middle East life which will not disappear whether one or a dozen American Secretaries of State come visiting. Emotion and the basic goal of revenge dominate the thought both of the unlettered and the ultra-sophisticated. Mohammed Hassenein Heikal is probably the Arab world's best journalist; he has been a confidant of the great and he has exercised great influence. When the Yom Kippur War broke out, he predicted that the Arabs would sweep to the pre-1967 lines and he asked rhetorically: "Then, at the next stage, will anything prevent them from liberating Palestine itself by force of arms?"

If hatred is complex, so are the wars it engenders. The Arab war against Israel, though grounded in furious hate, has among its driving forces such elements as inter-Arab rivalries and the ego compulsions of nations and their leaders. War, like hate, can be illogical; in the Arab war against Israel alliances can be made, broken and remade in a matter of months. War, like hatred, unites diverse forces in a common purpose—but it also results in quarrels about the tactics demanded. The Arab war against Israel unites feudal kings and revolutionaries, oil sheikhs and bankrupt presidents in determination to crush Israel, but it is too much to expect all of them to agree on every aspect of the war plan.

Hatred is something they all share, and the question of Israel's existence is so compelling an issue that it can divide them, enflame them, reunite them. In the 1967 war, Egypt, Syria and Jordan were allies. Within three years Syrian tanks were invading Jordan in a dispute over Palestinian rights. In 1972 Egypt broke relations with Jordan over tactics and principle in the war against Israel. In 1973 Jordan sent its best fighting units to help the Syrian-Egyptian offensive. Examples are easy to find. Thus, Iraq and Syria are forever involved in a dispute over Ba'ath Socialist ideology (and water rights) as bitter and deep as the Sino-Soviet dispute over Marxist theory (and frontiers). And yet Iraq rushed hundreds of tanks and thousands of soldiers to join the Syrian brethren when the crusade against Israel erupted into war again in 1973. Three years later, the brothers were at each other's throats once more, this time over the Palestinian cause (and power).

The tactics shift as the circumstances and the actors change. In broad terms, however, it is fair to say that in recent years the Arab world has divided into three groups with three distinct approaches to the problem of destroying Israel:

The rejectionists. The term was not invented by some inspired Western journalist. It is self-bestowed and those Arab states which use it to describe themselves are proud of it. An official newspaper in Baghdad said in the mid-1970s: "A rejectionist stand requires complete faith in the line of armed struggle for complete liberation." An official Iraqi statement, broadcast in 1975, bemoaned the fact that "more than a quarter century has passed since the usurpation of Palestine."

The rejectionists are quite literal and specific in their demands: Palestine was usurped, it must be freed. That means all of Palestine, not just part of the sacred homeland. Tactical compromises such as an "interim" state in part of Palestine as a stepping-stone toward the great goal are to be condemned, and Western suggestions for a more gradual diplomatic approach are to be shunned. A spokesman for the Ba'ath regime in Iraq said in the mid-1970s: "The Arabs must get away from humiliating settlements imposed by imperialism." Qaddafi of Libya put it more bluntly: "All attempts at settlement . . . by regionalists, secessionists, reactionaries, renegade elements . . . are inevitably drowned when the deluge comes." Until the day of liberation arrives, there can only be permanent confrontation, permanent war. "Armed struggle," as an Iraqi spokesman noted, had to be escalated. In addition to Libya and Iraq, the *rejection front* has included Algeria, parts of the Arab terror movement and one or two of the smaller Arab states.

The moderates. The Arabs themselves do not use this description. It is a Western invention, created by apologists who believe that, because *they* are moderate in their views on all things, there simply *must* be moderates all over the world, on every issue. In fact, a moderate fanatic remains a fanatic.

The principal Arab moderates, if that is the right term, have been Egypt as run by Anwar el-Sadat and Saudi Arabia under the rule of the al-Aziz family. Both regimes might more accurately be called pragmatic. Each has had a time problem. The Saudis have needed time to adjust to mastering the flood of complicated technological tools and advanced weaponry supplied by America before claiming their full and rightful role in the Middle East struggle. The Egyptians have needed time to rebuild an economy wrecked by war, mismanagement, corruption and an impossible birth rate. Each, therefore, has been ready for a productive pause in all-out confrontation.

That, however, does not presage settlement or peace.

61

The moderate position has a basis in cold logic. It was explained in part by Cairo's ambassador to Kuwait when he was asked why Egypt had accepted UN resolutions calling for a *peaceful* solution to the Arab-Israel conflict. "The wise man," the ambassador replied, "sets phases to reach his objective." It was perhaps better stated by the grand old man of Arab nationalism, Habib Bourguiba of Tunisia, who once gave this advice to his Arab brethren: "Take and demand." Sadat adapted this to: Take and demand—but make your demands *seem* reasonable and moderate. One step at a time, and be careful about your image.

The West either failed to understand Sadat's strategy or else closed its eyes. One day in November, 1975, Henry Kissinger told the World Affairs Council in Pittsburgh: "I think it is important to keep in mind the very vital role that President Sadat has played in helping to move the Middle East toward peace and moderation." On that same day, in Cairo, a columnist for the sober and authoritative newspaper *Al Ahram* wrote: "What is important is that Israel is experiencing a feeling of waning or 'withering.' This withering will not stop even if Israel withdraws to the 1967 borders, even if it recognizes the rights of the Palestinian people in the West Bank and Gaza, and even if it recognizes the PLO."

Whether Kissinger knew or cared, the Egyptian columnist was a close associate of Sadat. He was describing a definite, crystallized Arab strategy of war: Israel was to be weakened by economic and diplomatic warfare and by terrorist incursions, by the costs of constant semi-mobilization, by the drain of an arms race fueled by the endless billions of the Arab oil princes; Israel was then to be pushed back in one or more steps—by international action, probably combined with guerrilla warfare and almost certainly with an occasional flareup of classic warfare—to the 1967 frontiers; an Arab state was to be established in the vacated areas; that Arab state, with the help of its faithful brethren, was to drain the strength of the rump Israeli state and pave the way for an eventual take-over. In other words, the Arabs would take what they could get, pause but press while pausing, and then take some more. The process, involving much time and much patience, is sometimes known among the Arabs as "erosion," sometimes as "attrition."

This policy would deprive Israel of vital strategic space, and place the vast and newly equipped armies of its Arab neighbors within striking distance of its cities, farms and factories. It would also place an Arab statelet in half of Palestine. Some of the more image-conscious Arab leaders preferred not to talk about what would happen then. There were no such inhibitions within George Habash, of the well-financed, well-equipped Popular Front for the Liberation of Palestine. In 1976 Habash said: "In the last analysis the 'rejection front' would be prepared to take up arms against its fellow Palestinians if the authorities of any Palestinian West Bank state set up under a peace settlement tried to prevent the continuation of guerrilla action against Israel." He continued: "The 'rejection front' countries [Libya, Iraq, Algeria] would carry on an escalating struggle against any Arab state supporting a peaceful settlement with Israel on all levels except that of military conflict." Habash knew exactly where he stood and what he wanted; in 1974 he had told a Beirut newspaper: "There is a minimal Palestinian national solution. This minimum is the rejection of any recognition of the Zionist entity, a refusal to negotiate with it, and a strengthening of faith in our masses' ability to shatter this entity. We must clearly and openly declare our rejection of any settlement based on the continued existence of this foreign body."

The militants. The term is an arbitrary one, since there is

63

no generally accepted word to describe the policy adopted in recent years by Syria, Jordan and assorted allies. They believe in war, but not in constant war; they have not rejected diplomacy, but see it as a temporary, tactical weapon. They are somewhat less rigid than the *rejectionists* and just might accept new agreements worked out by middlemen but only on the most uncompromising terms, only in unison with Arab brothers and only as steps toward a final solution of the Israeli problem. To them, Egypt's independent decision to sign a second disengagement accord with Israel, minor though the "concessions" it contained might have seemed to the Israelis, raised the terrible spectre of a separate peace and a sellout of the cause of Palestine. It did not matter that, in fact, these fears were groundless. The accord, as seen through their eyes, represented a heresy so appalling and a splintering of the Arab front against Israel so traumatic as to lead inevitably to the upheaval in Lebanon.

Under that agreement, Israel surrendered oil fields and strategic passes. Egypt's only reciprocal concession of any concrete value permitted Israeli cargoes—not vessels—to pass through the Suez. An untrained listener to the Damascan radio's domestic—i.e., Arabic—service might have supposed, however, that this meant the world had come to an end. On the day the first ship bearing Israeli cargo entered the canal, Damascus broadcast: "Today the enemy ship passed through the Suez while the canal towns were sad and the bones of their martyrs were trembling with anger and even the canal water groaned with anger. . . . It is the first step toward coexistence with the enemy, toward shaking hands with the murderous hands, toward submissive and humiliating recognition of . . . the Zionist entity and toward forgiving all the crimes and disasters."

Each of the three groups uses words freely to demonstrate to the Arab public the efficacy of its tactics as opposed to the tactics of the others, the purity of its hatred, the totality of its devotion to the cause. Qaddafi of Libya had Sadat's disengagement accord in mind when he thundered: "The struggle between us and the Jews is one historic and inevitable struggle which has not been stopped by treaty or agreement." Sadat used the pragmatic argument to defend himself: "We have isolated Israel." The Voice of the Arabs, broadcasting from Cairo, will claim: "Egypt's policy is working to shake the foundations of Israel's existence." A joint Syrian-Libyan communique will reply: "Deviation from the line of confrontation and liberation and becoming involved [sic] in Zionist and imperialist plans means abandoning the national cause and following a mirage." When Syrian troops turned their guns on Palestinian gunmen in the war in Lebanon, Assad's sometimes ally, sometimes rival, Sadat of Egypt, voiced cruel criticism: "The entire Arab nation is losing. Only Israel is winning."

But these statements are, in part, public relations postures, in part tactics springing out of the frustration of Israel's continued stubborn existence. Tactics differ—Eisenhower and Montgomery had bitter tactical disputes during World War II—but the goal is shared. Saudi Arabia may have been in deep disagreement with a given Syrian or Jordanian move, but it still maintained a battalion of heavily armed troops in each of these confrontation states as part of its commitment to the joint battle. Qaddafi of Libya has proved himself capable of castigating Sadat and then, almost immediately afterward, lending him aircraft to fight the Israelis.

To a large extent, it is simply a question of style, of deciding whether to use words as rapiers or bludgeons. In 1974, while Sadat was hustling the moderate line abroad,

Egypt's only political party issued a proclamation saying: "The struggle between Egypt and the Arab world on the one side and Zionism on the other side is a struggle between two different civilizations and therefore a struggle for generations." On March 24, 1976, at the 1,897th meeting of the UN Security Council, Libya's blunt delegate addressed the question of Israel's existence and said: "This racist entity in the Middle East must be destroyed and it will be destroyed one day."

In essence, there is no difference between the two positions.

5

The Useful Refugees

The end of the 1948 war between Israel and the Arab states found the Egyptian army short of its goal of Tel Aviv but in possession of a strategic sliver of land. Barely five miles wide by twenty-five miles long, it ran along the coast from the Sinai border almost to the site of the ancient biblical city of Ashkelon. It soon became known as the Gaza Strip, and it was itself to become a *casus belli*.

The strip was a patchwork of citrus groves, villages, empty stretches of desert and one fair-sized town, Gaza. The war had trebled the population and the Strip was jammed with people. Work and homes for the refugees could be provided only through investments. But Cairo had no intention of making Gaza economically viable or permitting the refugees to move on to Egyptian territory. They were to remain frozen in time and space because a special role had been chosen for them. It was the intention of the Arab states, said Egypt's Foreign Minister in 1949, that the refugees "shall return as masters of the homeland, not as

67

slaves. More explicitly, they intend to annihilate the State of Israel."

Until that moment in the future, they were of little concern to Cairo. Jobless, the refugees lived in camps with no electricity, no piped water, no hope of improvement. The American novelist and reporter Martha Gellhorn visited the Strip in 1969—twenty-one years after the war—and wrote in *The Atlantic Monthly* that Gaza "is not a hell-hole, not a visible diaster. It is worse. It is a jail." It was only one of many.

Fully a quarter-century after that first war, *The Congressional Quarterly* was to state: "The Arab leaders refused to absorb them [the refugees] on the grounds that their lands lacked resources and were already overpopulated and that resettlement would imply the permanence of Israel." There was, in fact, abundant room—in Syria, Iraq, Libya and elsewhere. But, as Cairo radio put it ten years after the first of the wars with Israel, the refugees were "the cornerstone of the Arabs' struggle against Israel . . . the refugees are the armament of the Arabs and Arab nationalism." In countries where identity papers are vital, the refugees had no passports, no citizenship, no resident visas, no political rights. To this day, they are sojourners in the Arab world.

Jordan gave them legitimacy. But Jordan was unique. The other Arab states were functioning units when the war came, and the conflict produced no changes in their status. The 1948 war transformed Jordan from a sleepy desert fiefdom with a predominately nomadic bedouin population into a kingdom on both sides of the Jordan River with rich cities, fertile farms and a varied populace. In annexing the West Bank, Jordan gained material and human resources of considerable value. Jordan proclaimed the refugees as Jordanian, but Jordan, too, made no effort to give them new roots. They were to dream of reconquest and, in the meantime, they lived in tin huts.

The world assumed that the problem was temporary. The UN voted Arab refugee relief as an emergency measure for one year. A UN commission of experts proposed a set of works programs aimed at economic integration, but the Arab host governments—Egypt, Jordan, Lebanon, Syria— sabotaged the whole idea. The UN then offered a $200 million program of resettlement and rehabilitation, but it was smothered at birth. Only $7 million was ever used. The UN proposed that refugees be resettled in Libya, in Syria, in the oasis region of El 'Arish in northern Sinai; the Arabs refused. The Eisenhower administration mapped a detailed program to harness the Jordan River and to create land for refugee resettlement; the Arabs killed the plan. The United Nations Relief and Works Agency for Palestine refugees (UNRWA) ended up each year spending its millions on relief, almost nothing on "works." A ranking UNRWA official left his job in frustration and said: "The Arab states do not want to solve the refugee problem. They want to keep it as an open sore, as an affront to the United Nations and as a weapon against Israel. Arab leaders don't give a damn whether the refugees live or die." Gradually, the world got the message: the Arab refugees were on welfare.

Dr. Elfan Rees, adviser on refugees to the World Council of Churches, wrote in a 1957 report: ". . . Political issues aside, the Arab refugee problem is by far the easiest postwar refugee problem to solve by integration. By faith, language, race and social organization, they are indistinguishable from their fellows in their host countries. There is room for them, in Syria and Iraq. There is a developing demand for the kind of manpower they represent. More unusually still, there is the money to make this integration possible. The UN General Assembly, five years ago, voted a sum of $200 million to provide, and here I quote the phrase, 'homes and jobs' for the Arab refugees. That money remains unspent, not because these tragic people are strangers in a strange land, because they are not, not because there is no room for them to be established, because there is, but simply for political reasons. . . .''

When the Arabs became refugees, many of them were following instructions—from Arab radio stations, local notables and leaders of the Arab world. They were told to leave, to give the Arab armies fighting room and to disrupt the Jewish economy; they obeyed their instructions. Some left their homes in organized convoys, some quietly on their own, some in panic. In Haifa, the "Arab National Committee" rejected a truce offer as a "disgrace" and demanded transfer to neighboring Arab countries. The rich often did not even bother to pack away their household goods. Those who left, the Greek Catholic Archbishop of Galilee recalled later, were "confident" that they would return "within a week or two. Their leaders had promised them that the Arab armies would crush the 'Zionist gangs' very quickly and that there would be no . . . fear of a long exile.'' And they were going to kinsfolk or brother Arabs; all would be well.

Soon enough, the refugees realized that the Arab armies had failed; they were furious at the Arab League and Arab leadership but could only turn their fury inward. "The Arab governments," a Palestinian bitterly wrote in a Jordanian newspaper several years later, "told us, 'Get out so we can get in.' So we got out, but they did not get in." The rich fitted easily into the life of Beirut or Amman; the skilled found productive work; the resourceless were trapped in camps and grew accustomed to weekly rations, red tape and identity cards. But many camp dwellers became adept at exploiting the bureaucratic rules. Births were duly registered; deaths were not. Funerals were held quietly, and the ration cards of the dead were hidden. Ration cards were forged. "There are refugees," the UNRWA director noted, "who hold as many as five hundred ration cards." People with no papers at all appeared at UN camps and claimed to be refugees; the result was chaos. Local friends and relations often ended up with ration cards.

The Arab states were not paying for the rations—the West was. And the more refugees there appeared to be, the stronger the Arab case would be. From the beginning, the Arab states played the numbers game. No one had counted the Palestinians as they left their homes, but the Arabs categorically declared there were one million refugees. The only reliable statistics were the population registers of the British mandatory government. Poring over these detailed tables, demographers concluded that no more than 500,000 Arabs had left the territories which became Israel. And yet, in 1950, 960,000 Arabs were officially registered with UNRWA as refugees.

The camps became a way of life. As one observer noted, refugees who found jobs were pressured to stay in the camps because there they would serve as reminders that Israel must be returned to Arab rule. A child born in the camps was considered, by UNRWA decree, to be a "refugee." By the 1970s there were *three generations* of refugees, and the number of registered refugees had trebled.

The children born in the camps were taught hate. UNRWA paid for the schools and the Arab governments approved text books studded with anti-Israel and anti-Semitic propaganda. An expert commission appointed by UNESCO's Director-General in 1967 reported that in UNRWA schools "an excessive importance is given to the problem of relations between the prophet Mohammed and the Jews of Arabia, in terms tending to convince young people that the Jewish community as a whole has always been and always will be the irreconcilable enemy of the

Moslem community.'' In geography and history books "the term Israel is never used. . . . The Territories constituting the State of Israel are frequently designated as the 'usurped portion of Palestine.' '' The books in use employed "the deplorable language of anti-Semitism" and the student exercises "are often inspired by a preoccupation with indoctrination against Jews rather than by strict educationalism." (A sample: when the Israelis captured the Gaza Strip in 1967, they found an art exhibit on the walls of a school for girls in a refugee camp. It consisted of drawings of Israeli soldiers and male civilians attacking Arab women.)

By 1954 Egypt was ready to make use of the camp generation it had raised on this diet of hatred. The decision was taken to launch terror raids from Gaza into Israel. Refugees were organized into terror squads and given a name, *fedayeen*, literally those who sacrifice themselves; the fanaticism was already there. Trained by Egyptian officers, supervised by the Egyptian army chief of intelligence for the Strip, they were sent to attack farm villages, ambush cars, plant mines. On one foray they slaughtered six Israeli children participating in a synagogue service. The then commander of the UN Truce Supervision Organization, a Canadian general, considered the *fedayeen* attacks "a war crime." But their work, it developed later, was seed-work, a cherished example for another generation of terrorists. From these simple beginnings, Arab terrorism moved on to the blowing up of civilian aircraft, the distribution of booby-traps and letter bombs, the tossing of Israeli children from third-story apartment windows to death and the bloodbath at the Munich Olympics in 1972.

The Arab refugees are a phenomenon among the tens of millions of refugees of this tragic century. There were:

Two million Greeks, Turks and Bulgarians after World War I.

72

Nearly seven million Germans from the Prussian provinces in the East after World War II.

Eleven to fourteen million Hindus and Moslems in the traumatic division of the Indian subcontinent.

One million Koreans as a result of civil war.

One million French *colons* as a by-production of Algerian independence.

One million mainland Chinese in flight to Hong Kong.

All were resettled, except the Palestinians.

The picture is dramatically different on the other side of the Arab-Israeli confrontation line. In the first difficult years of statehood, Israel's every resource was strained by the need to absorb 255,000 Jewish refugees from Arab persecution in addition to the flood of survivors from Nazi Europe. By the mid-1950s, the number of Jews in flight from the Arabs more than equaled the number of Arabs who had left Israel. But the Jews of the Arab world were not the victims of a shooting war; they fled after the imposition by every Arab state of repressive laws and measures and regulations directed only at Jews.

The Jewish community of Iraq, its roots stretching back to the biblical exile by the Waters of Babylon, was virtually destroyed in a matter of months. The exodus began in 1949—a black year for Jews all over the Middle East—with slaughter in the streets of Baghdad and the looting of businesses owned by Jews. By the time the Jews were ready to venture forth from their shuttered houses again, there was little to justify the risk. The Iraqi government had taken a leaf from *Mein Kampf* and was busily engaged in some familiar measures. Jews were summarily fired from the civil service. Jewish children were barred from schools. Hospitals were closed to Jews. While the stunned Jewish community was still trying to tutor its children, doctor its sick in makeshift clinics and support its jobless, the next blow fell.

Hundreds of Jews were rounded up and hauled off to prison on phony charges or on no charges at all. Emigration was enthusiastically encouraged and more than 110,000 Jews of the 135,000 in Iraq fled to Israel. Those remaining were mercilessly squeezed, their community organizations outlawed, their professional lives restricted, their personal assets under constant audit. In an act of sheer terrorism, there was the public hanging, in 1969, of nine Jews condemned on trumped-up charges. Thousands flocked to this grisly event and howled hatred as the nine hooded figures dangled and jerked on their ropes. Three years later, there was another wave of arrests and eighteen Jews disappeared into the dungeons. They have never been accounted for, and the few hundred Jews who still live in Iraq do not ask.

Syria began harassing its Jews the moment the French left after World War II, before the UN had even voted to establish a Jewish state. Jews were banned from employment in government, public corporations and banks, harassed at work, attacked in the streets. Legal emigration became increasingly difficult, then virtually impossible, and government officials feathered their nests at the expense of those who could afford to pay heavily for exit papers. Most slipped out of the country illegally, leaving everything behind. The last of Syria's 45,000 Jews, some 3,000 luckless souls, were forced into ghettoes in Damascus, Aleppo and a single rural town, Kamishli. Their telephones were cut off. Jewish doctors and dentists were allowed to treat only Jewish patients. Forbidden to travel more than five kilometers (less than three miles) from their ghetto homes, all carried identity cards labeling them in red letters as Jews; these cards had to be shown on entering and leaving the tiny neighborhoods into which they were compressed. In Kamishli, the doors of the houses in the ghetto were marked in big red letters: *of the Mosaic faith.* Kamishli was the home

74

of a new group of Syrian Jews, the professional beggars; they had trades, but both work and food were beyond the five-kilometer limit, out of bounds. It was easy enough to see what the Jews of Syria had lost, more difficult to assess the loss to Syria of its hard-working and skilled Jews. An example: with its Jews, Syria lost most of the gifted workmen who had lovingly crafted the wonderful silver inlay which was the rarest and most beautiful form of damascene. In the mid-1970s, the pressures on the few remaining Jews were apparently relaxed—ever so slightly and as a part of a campaign in the West to demonstrate Syrian "moderation."

In 1956, after the Suez war, a wave of xenophobia swept through Egypt. It was encouraged and fed by Gamal Abdel Nasser and his fellow officers—among them Anwar el-Sadat—of the new Egypt. Jews of foreign citizenship were treated like foreigners—all were forcibly expelled with little more than the clothes on their backs; if it was an indiscriminate gesture, it is possible to say that it was also non-discriminatory. Not so the treatment of the indigenous Jewish community which had chosen to remain in Egypt after the establishment of Israel eight years earlier. Many, following the Sinai flareup, were summarily deprived of Egyptian citizenship. Their community institutions were closed, their freedom of movement restricted, their ability to work narrowed. If that was not enough, the hapless Jews were the targets of unremitting anti-Semitic fulminations from the pen of Johann von Leers, an expert whose last employer had been the Ministry of Propaganda of the Third Reich. Von Leers provided vast piles of cartoons and hate material for the press, and his office churned out masses of venom for incorporation in school texts and pamphlets.

By 1967, the year of the Egyptian defeat in the Six-Day War, there were only 2,500 Jews left in all of Egypt. Hundreds were thrown into prison during the war, among them the heads of virtually every remaining Jewish family. Some were cruelly tortured, many were held in isolation, their disorientation compounded by fear for their families. Most left the country three years later when the Egyptian regime finally bowed to international pressure and permitted their emigration.

The vast Arab East is almost empty of Jews today. Of the 761,000 thousand who lived in Arab countries in 1948, barely 50,000 remain, and 35,000 of them are in a single country, Morocco, home in 1948 to 240,000 Jews.

In 1973, the most recent year when reliable estimates were made, the Jewish community of Algeria—whose regime is one of the most ardent supporters of the PLO concept of one Arab state in Palestine—was down from 130,000 in 1948 to 1,000. Of Egypt's 65,000 Jews, 400 remained. Of Iraq's 130,000, another 400. Qaddafi's Libya, once home for 38,000, had twenty Jews left.

There had, in effect, been an exchange of populations in refugees, a fact which the Arabs find infinitely unsettling. Although they make a great deal of Israel's insistence that the refugee question can be dealt with only within an overall peace settlement, they themselves expropriated the property of their fleeing Jews and formally closed the doors against their return.

In 1970, a representative of the Syrian-supported Saiqa branch of the PLO told colleagues that this had been a historic error because, in barring their return to Arab countries, the Arabs had "made the Jews think constantly for twenty years that the sea is before them and the enemy behind, and that there was no recourse but to fight to defend their lives. . . ." He added, that with the establishment of an Arab Palestinian state which would replace Israel,

". . . many of them will chose to live outside Palestine. . . ."

Late in 1975, revolutionary Iraq became the first Arab country to invite its former Jewish citizens to return. And Baghdad radio carried a grateful cable from the Sons of the Jewish Community, the official spokesman for the 400 Jews remaining in that police state. The cable, signed by the organization's acting head, was addressed to President Ahmed Hassan al-Bakr and Vice Chairman Saddam Hussein of the Revolution Command Council. It stated :

> I wish to convey to your excellencies our greatest thanks and gratitude for the issuance of your historic revolutionary decision allowing Iraqi Jews—from whom Iraqi citizenship had been lifted—to return to Iraq, their dear homeland in which they and their forefathers had lived for a period of well over 2,500 years.
> This blessed decision has reinforced equality among the various religions, rejected all forms of racial and religious discrimination and truly expressed the principles of the government and its leader party—the Socialist Arab Ba'ath Party.
> On behalf of the Jewish community . . . we pledge to you and to the leader party that we will remain always and forever attached to the soil of this dear homeland and sincere to it and to the government of the revolution. . . .

History has its other ironies. After the 1967 war, some 600,000 Arab refugees fell into Israeli hands. Israel had to choose between two policies—to wall the conquered Arabs up as hostile security risks or to open the borders between Israel and the Arab areas to free commerce in people and goods. It chose the latter course. On occasion, Israel has paid in blood for that decision, but the results are a matter of record. Tens of thousands of refugees found work in Israel. Unemployment among the camp dwellers disappeared for the first time in memory. Men in the Gaza Strip who had, quite literally, not worked since 1948 found jobs.

By the 1970s, in fact, the Palestinian refugees were no longer such an aching problem. Not even Arab politicians can control the impact of time. More and more refugees have learned to mold their own fate. A hundred thousand or more are working in the Arab crescent from Libya to the Gulf. Many thousands have emigrated to the West, built new lives there and are no different now from Italian, British or East European newcomers in the United States, Canada and Australia. Most have rooted themselves somehow; even UNRWA statistics, which neutrals suspect because they are compiled by Palestinian UNRWA employees eager to prove a political case, show that little more than one quarter of the registered refugees live in the camps —458,000 out of 1,632,000 in 1975. As the UN itself has pointed out, some of the camps have developed into "thriving communities," some have become part of nearby cities. More than half the Arabs with official "refugee" status are citizens of Jordan and therefore do not share the one element which makes a person classically a refugee—statelessnesss. Indeed, only a quarter of the refugees registered with the UN now live outside the original borders of mandated Palestine.

As a human problem, the refugee issue is slowly disappearing. As a political issue, it is being kept alive artificially and with malice by Arab politicians and by the Palestine Liberation Organization. Deliberately, they try to present a false picture to the world—one that depicts all Palestinians as refugees from their native soil (in fact, 1.5 million live within the pre-1948 borders of Palestine) or as compelled to exist in the misery of the camps. Each year UNRWA's existence is renewed automatically by the pro-Arab majority at the UN. UNRWA's bureaucracy (mainly Palestinian) constantly emphasizes the despair to be found in the camps, the hopelessness of refugee life, and thus perpetuates what is, from their point of view, a useful myth. For, without refugees, the charge of Israeli injustice and usurpation would be empty. Without refugees, there would be no candidates for membership in the terror organizations. Without refugee camps the terrorists would lose their principal logistic bases. So, in every way possible, the folk memory of Palestine is sustained and the refugee status is zealously guarded. The culprits are always the Jews of Israel, never Arab leaders or the Arab rich.

The refugees have remained a tool to be used against Israel. In 1961, Gamal Abdel Nasser gloated: "If the Arabs return to Israel, Israel will cease to exist." Fifteen years later, nothing had changed politically; the Voice of the Arabs, broadcasting in Arabic out of Cairo, spoke of projecting the Palestine issue "in its true image, as a pan-Arab issue . . . not an issue of refugees or a human issue."

The point was nicely illustrated on June 8, 1976, when the Libyan Government bought a full page in the *Christian Science Monitor* to print the text of a new law "on encouragement of Arab experiences." The aim of the detailed statute was to attract skilled Arab workmen to the oil-rich but forbidding desert land as long-term residents or immigrants, and there were all sorts of generous come-ons—customs exemptions, free transport for the skilled hands, their families and their household goods, settlement subsidies, health insurance, guaranteed salaries until work could be found. But the law also contained this uncompromising clause: "The provisions concerning immigration for the purpose of naturalization . . . shall not be applicable to Palestinians." To Libya's dedicated rulers, it was vital that the Palestinians remain stateless, pawns of politics, twenty-eight years after their flight.

UNRWA's annual report makes interesting reading. In the quarter-century beginning in 1950, the report shows, UNRWA operations cost a total of $1,095,000,000, or much more than would have been needed to replace every refugee tin hut with a permanent dwelling, more than would have been needed to create jobs for hundreds of thousands of refugees. UNRWA is dependent upon donations from UN member states. Out of that impressive one billion plus total, the United States donated $619 million, Britain gave $138 million, Israel provided $6,776,000. The Soviet Union, which generously supports the Arab war against Israel, donated zero rubles. The entire Arab world, in that quarter-century, donated to UNRWA a combined total of $42 million for the care and feeding of brother Arabs. The oil State of Abu Dhabi gave $190,000, the emirate of Bahrein gave $73,867, Dubai gave $40,000, Oman $95,000 and the People's Democratic Republic of Yemen provided a generous $750. Algeria, rich in oil, rich in natural gas, rich in anti-Zionist rhetoric, gave nothing.

Every year the Arab belligerents arrayed against Israel contribute some $85 million for terror in the name of Palestine. In twenty-five years, they gave to the Palestinian refugees for whose cause they weep a grand total of just less than half that sum.

6

The Uses of Terror

*It is, finally, the day of victory. The last Arab-Israeli war
is over and even the laden looters of four invading armies
are weary of picking through the litter of Israel's silent,
smoking cities. The new Premier of Palestine has made his
appearance at the former Knesset building in Jerusalem and
is now praying at the Aksa mosque in the Old City. The
roundup of Zionist invaders has begun—those alien Jews
who, under the constitution of the Palestine Liberation Organization, must be expelled from the new democratic and
secular state of Palestine.*

*The cut-off date is 1917. Anyone who arrived after that
date must go. Everyone who came into Israel from the death
camps of Europe must go. Everyone who fled in 1948 from
Egypt, Syria, Libya, Morocco, Yemen and Iraq must go.*

*Prime Minister Yitzhak Rabin must go. President
Ephraim Katzir must go, and Motte Gur, the army chief of
staff; Avraham Harman, the president of the Hebrew University, must go, and so must Abba Eban; Teddy Kollek,
the mayor of Jerusalem, must go.*

If Martin Buber were still alive, he would have to go, as would S. J. Agnon, who won a Nobel Prize for literature, and E. L. Sukenik, the archaeologist who identified the Dead Sea scrolls, and Chaim Weizmann.

Golda Meir must go. Ninety-five per cent of the population of Israel must go.

Article VI of the PLO constitution, the Palestine National Covenant, is the background for that incredible scenario. It states:

"The Jews who had normally resided in Palestine until the beginning of the Zionist invasion will be considered Palestinian."

In a formal resolution interpreting the Covenant, the PLO set the date of "the Zionist invasion" at 1917. Jews who descended from those who arrived after that date or who themselves entered the country during or after the British mandate are, therefore, no part of the Palestine population.

The Palestine National Covenant is not readily available in the West—Arab propagandists prefer to distribute more upbeat material—but the Arabic original can be found in any Arab capital. It is a matter of record, and its language is, by the standards of the region and of revolutionary rhetoric, quite clear and to the point. It states, among other things:

> The partition of Palestine in 1947 and the establishment of the state of Israel are entirely illegal. . . . The liberation of Palestine, from an Arab viewpoint, is a national duty. . . . Accordingly, the Arab nation must mobilize all its military, human, moral and spiritual capabilities to participate actively with the people of Palestine in the liberation of Palestine. . . . Armed struggle is the only way to liberate Pales-

82

tine. . . . Thus, it is an overall strategy, not merely a tactical phase. . . . Commando action constitutes the nucleus
of the Palestine popular liberation War. This requires its escalation. . . .

The PLO was created not by the masses in an upsurge of
nationalistic fervor but by the leaders of the Arab states in a
calculated geopolitical move. The operative decision was
taken not by secret council of burning revolutionaries but
by an Arab summit convened in 1964 by Gamal Abdel
Nasser of Egypt. A "Palestinian National Congress" was
then organized for the formal task of proclaiming the PLO
and adopting the Covenant; it was held later that year in the
Old City of Jerusalem, then rigorously controlled by King
Hussein's tough police regime. The "congress" was inspired, organized, financed and run by the League of Arab
States. The PLO's leadership was selected by the Arab
League; its budget was provided by the League.

Leadership and ideology were created, too. Thus, in
1956, a Palestinian notable named Achmed Shukairy addressed the UN General Assembly and, echoing a recurrent
theme in the Levant where clearly delineated nation-states
in the modern Western sense dated only from the collapse
of the far-flung Turkish Empire in the closing phases of
World War I, announced that "it is common knowledge
that Palestine is nothing but southern Syria." Eight years
later Shukairy was hand-picked to be the PLO's first chairman and he dutifully set about peddling a different line.

At first, the creation was neglected. The Israeli soldiers
who fought their way through the suburbs of Old Jerusalem
in the 1967 war found the PLO's international headquarters—a small cottage on a dusty lane, equipped with a few
desks, one or two typewriters, a couple of telephones and
heaps of particularly repulsive anti-Semitic propaganda

badly printed on cheap paper. After the war, however, the Arab states, their armies shattered, in need of alternative weapons against Israel, saw the inestimable value of terror and the political and public relations potential of such code phrases as "national liberation" and "legitimate national rights."

The coffers were opened. And after a time money gushed forth in such quantities that, as a Princeton professor of Near Eastern studies put it, Arab generosity had made the PLO "the wealthiest revolutionary movement in history." Tens of millions of dollars a year were not too much for the few thousand bureaucrats and killers of the PLO. After the outrageous terrorist attack in Munich in 1972, Libya's Qaddafi gave one splinter group a $5 million bonus. The belligerent Arab nations provided everything the PLO required—arms, intelligence information, operational contact, training bases, passports, diplomatic cover and use of the diplomatic pouch, broadcasting studios, radio wavelengths and other propaganda facilities, political and diplomatic support, public relations advice and aid, and in time, political status.

Acts of terror were so evidently an important part of the overall program that they were subjected to academic scrutiny. J. Bowyer Bell of Columbia University, in his study *Transnational Terror,* concluded that the acts of terror fell into two principal categories. One type of action, such as the bloodbath at Lod Airport in which Arab-directed Japanese terrorists killed twenty-five people and wounded fifty-six others, was aimed at *strategic advantage:* "The major function of spraying machine gun fire into a transit lounge is not the elimination of the immediate victims, but rather the general intimidation of all potential visitors to Israel." The second category consisted of acts of *symbolic terror,* as exemplified by the murder of eleven Israeli Olympic athletes, symbolically a victory over the very finest physical specimens the country could produce. Bell was theorizing about acts which, at least in the minds of their planners, had purpose, not the ever more frequent outbursts of pointless murder with no motivation beyond hate.

(Bell also pointed to a grim phenomenon, the "revolutionary milieu that . . . encourages the exchange of aid and comfort" among terrorists of a variety of countries and cultures. Arab terrorists, backed as they were by governments, appeared to dominate this informal but potent network. On friendly soil they trained members of the German Baader-Meinhof group and other specialists in violent death. In turn, the Japanese terrorists en route to Lod Airport picked up forged identity documents in Frankfurt and weapons in Rome. German and Arab terrorists worked hand in hand in mid-1976 to hijack that Tel Aviv–Paris airbus and direct it to Uganda's Entebbe Airport.)

Over the years, relations between patrons and clients grew complex and incestuous. Each of the revolutionary subgroups developed its techniques, its ideology and its special friend or friends among the Arab states. Yasir Arafat's al-Fatah was blessed with Saudi aid; the Arab Liberation Front was maintained by Iraq; the Popular Front for the Liberation of Palestine General Command had links with Libya; Saiqa (Thunderbolt) was Syria's private property, financed, trained and directed by the Syrian army. All prospered, gathering arms and funds and prestige and influence.

Rival Arab leaders and nations used the Palestinian revolutionaries as a convenience and as an instrument in power struggles, and were used in turn. But the price grew high. In sowing terror and bankrolling the PLO, which endlessly preached death to the Jews, the Arab states raised whirlwind after whirlwind. The men of al-Fatah became a law

85

unto themselves in Jordan, extorting "contributions," defying authority, roaming the land with their guns, until finally they threatened King Hussein's throne. To save himself, he drove them out in a blood-drenched military action. President Nemery of Sudan, though thoroughly committed to the PLO cause, felt deeply insulted when terrorists killed the American ambassador and two other diplomats in his capital—and he bluntly accused Arafat's al-Fatah of the deed. When Arab terrorists dared import their tactics to Damascus and briefly held ninety hostages in an abortive attack on a downtown hotel, they were hanged within twenty-four hours before a large crowd, and other thousands, including busloads of schoolchildren, came to view their bodies swaying from ropes at a busy intersection; President Assad was quoted as saying the men were criminals who acted as if they were in Israel. The infectious fever of lawlessness, machismo and religious hate spread from the armed Palestinians to the Lebanese, raging through the country and breeding havoc. In Lebanon, as earlier in Jordan, the terrorists, intoxicated by guns and Western publicity, committed the sin of *hubris*, overweening pride. They forgot that the movement was simply a weapon to be subordinated to overall strategy and to the needs of sovereign states. They had to be cut down to manageable size.

And yet through all the ugliness, the internecine murders, the anarchy, the blood-lust, the attacks on school buses and civilian aircraft, the use of hatchets as well as button mines and SAM-missiles to kill civilians, the deaths of thousands in civil conflict—the subsidies from Arab treasuries to the PLO continued to flow copiously. Political support for the cause of Palestine remained fervent. No Arab state ever voiced an objection to the doctrine embodied in the Palestine National Covenant and all it meant. None rejected the concept of armed violence to cleanse Palestine. All supported the concept of the total Arabization of the land between the Mediterranean and the Jordan. None scorned the concept of separating all but the pre-1917 Jewish settlers and their sons from the land. As for the PLO, a body given to much discussion, nowhere on the record—at no forum, at none of its frequent congresses, in none of its journals—has it ever repudiated Article VI of the Covenant or the 1917 cut-off date. They remained operative against the day when, as Arafat told Arab youth training in Syria in 1974, their generation "will reach the sea and hoist the flag of Palestine over Tel Aviv."

But all this was within the family. To the West, the armed men and their sponsors usually offered other themes. One was embodied in Arafat's inaugural speech to the United Nations General Assembly. He was there because the sovereign Arab states had put him there. But he carried with him an image of renunciation—no private life, no interest in money, possessions or what he eats, no purpose except the movement's welfare. And in his checkered headdress and his khaki uniform, with his unshaven chin and his air of intensity, he was a figure of charismatic mystery. Standing before the awed delegates with a holster at his shoulder, he made a memorable statement: In one hand, he warned, he held an olive branch, and in the other a gun.

"Do not let the olive branch fall from my hand," Yasir Arafat told his transfixed audience.

In psychological terms, this game has been called "Now look what you've made me do." According to this thinking, there would be no violence if only the Israelis would have the decency to commit national suicide. Article XXII of the Palestine National Covenant puts it this way: ". . . the liberation of Palestine will liquidate the Zionist and imperialist presence and bring about the stabilization of peace in the Middle East."

The other principal theme, offered in full seriousness,

was brotherhood. Gone was the early PLO slogan, "We will drive the Jews into the sea!" That had been the work of Ahmed Shukairy, the first PLO chairman. He turned out a failure and the Arab League replaced him after the Six-Day War. Shukairy's slogan, the Arab states agreed, was offensive and reminiscent of the disastrous sabre-rattling which had precipitated the war. And, as public relations experts in London and New York pointed out, it was in unfortunate conformity with the Israeli view of the situation. In adopting that ugly slogan, Hafez al-Assad of Syria sadly admitted years later, "we were rendering great service to Israel." The new slogan was designed to project a blander image to a very large number of people. It was for everyone. It was: *"A Democratic Palestinian State."*

Many of the terrorists were horrified when this new tactical approach was first offered in the late 1960s. The cafés of Beirut were filled with agitated men in hot debate on the projected switch.

It was so much a matter of concern that the sober Beirut newspaper, *Al Anwar,* sponsored a symposium of *fedayeen* spokesmen to discuss the issue in depth. *Al Anwar* published the deliberations in full, back in the days when Beirut was a peaceful city, and Yehoshafat Harkabi, a noted Israeli Arab-watcher, quoted extensively from the proceedings in his study, *Palestinians and Israel.*

The symposium dealt with the implications of the new slogan and how that political catch-phrase could be assimilated into the actual intentions of the terror groups. In addition, it examined the logistic problems it might create, since the concept might bind the Arabs to enfranchise a dangerous Jewish minority.

The more extreme groups, such as the Iraqi-controlled Arab Liberation Front, dismissed the slogan out of hand because any separate Palestine state, democratic or otherwise, was an additional stumbling block to the national revolutionary struggle for Arab unity (i.e., from Morocco to Yemen). The fate of the Israeli population was of no more interest than the position of other minorities in the Middle East—"denominational or others." All, the ALF spokesman said grandly, would have equal rights in the new order. It was not clear whether Iraq, a particularly quarrelsome country with a record of black intolerance toward any minority, would be willing to erase its own boundaries in this visionary new world.

Even the ALF delegate, however, conceded the propaganda value of the new slogan as a sop to "progressive opinion and the world left movement." In this, he was joined by the spokesman of the PLO itself, who agreed that the phrase was "a successful slogan and a useful political and propaganda act." An ally from al-Fatah explained that the new line was intended to "tell the world that the objective of the Palestinians and the Arabs is not to throw the Jews into the sea but to liquidate the Zionist state and establish a new state."

Even so, it was the consensus of the gathering that the slogan was too dangerous to use, even as a stratagem. The phrase carried with it implications of coexistence with the Jews that were far from the intent of the participants. If the goal of a democratic state were to replace the goal of driving the Jews into the sea, what was an Arab state going to do with all those Jews?

The PLO delegate thought the Jews should be told that they must return to the countries from which they had come and there "seek another way of striving for a solution to what is called 'the problem of persecuted Jews in the world.'" The representative from Syrian-backed Saiqa said he no longer thought, as he had five years earlier, that it was proper to slaughter the Jews; he was sure they yearned for their old homes, particularly in Arab countries, and he hoped that the Arab states would permit them to return when the time came.

There were other, terrible, specters raised by the new slogan, and the ALF man wanted nothing to do with it even as a tactical step because ". . . if Israel agrees to it, the sponsors of the idea will *have to accept it. . . .*" [*italics added*] The representative of the Democratic Front was quick to reassure him: "As for the question concerning what will happen if Israel agrees . . . , the answer is: Israel will not agree to this slogan, and it is impossible [for Israel] to agree, because it means elimination of the state of Israel. . . ."

In spite of the doubts expressed at the Beirut symposium, the PLO saw the urgent need for a new image and eventually adopted the revised slogan. There was a single change, again for reasons of public relations. The slogan as it now stands calls for the replacement of Israel by "a democratic and secular Palestinian state."

The PLO, it happens, is not simply the umbrella organization of a series of disparate terror groups; it is also the creation of the Arab states which supply and support it. Not one of these states, with the questionable exception of Lebanon before its civil war, is either democratic or secular. They are dictatorships or monarchies exercising varying degrees of tyranny. They are Islamic theocracies whose constitutions open with a declaration of the Moslem character of the state. (Saudi Arabia has no consitution beyond the Koran. Iraq, according to its constitution, is an "Arab, Islamic, independent and sovereign republic.") In each, Islamic law is the basis of the law of the state and in some Islamic law is the *only* law. Jordan, Libya and Tunisia vary greatly in their economy and government, but the constitution of each contains the exact same words: "Islam is the religion of the state."

Yasir Arafat, who dreamed of presiding over the Democratic and Secular State of Palestine which would replace Israel, was himself strongly bound to Islam; and al-Fatah, his power base, worked in its purely practical early phase with a jingoistic Moslem grouping called "The Worshippers of the All-Merciful." Arafat's *nom de guerre*, Abu Ammar, was recognized by all Moslems as the name of Mohammed's strong right arm, a noted warrior of crusading Islam. The name al-Fatah was derived from a root word with connotations of *jihad*. The units of the regular Palestine Liberation Army were named for historic Moslem victories over the infidel, Christian Crusader and pagan alike. Even Arafat's figures of speech and the charges he hurled against the "Zionists" were strikingly reminiscent of Koranic verses and allied commentary vilifying Jews.

Thus, when the Italian journalist Oriana Fallaci urged Arafat to be "fair" and to acknowledge the bravery of Israel's soldiers, he replied: "No! No! No! They aren't brave at all. In a face-to-face fight, they aren't even soldiers. . . . They always seek out the weakest targets. . . . They never move unless they are sure that everything will go well, and if it doesn't, they never stand their ground." The Koran, as quoted at the Fourth Islamic Conference, makes much the same point: "God the Almighty has notified us of the extent of their [the Jews'] military preparations which were the outcome of their dismay, cowardice and feebleness when they encountered true Believers face-to-face. . . . They will not fight against you in a body save in fortified villages or from behind walls. . . ." (LIX, 13-1)

Arafat also alluded to the Israelis' reluctance to sacrifice themselves in battle, in contrast to the reckless disregard for life shown by his men. "They are too scared to die to show any courage," he told Fallaci contemptuously, adding that "we don't worry about dying." The Koran, in a statement endlessly quoted in the Arab world, states: "Thou

91

wilt indeed find them [the Jews] of all people most greedy of life." Islam regards death in *jihad* as sanctification, while the Jewish respect for preservation of life is a mark of despicable cowardice. Constant repetition of this Koranic preachment was part of the conditioning of young Arab terrorists. Their very name, *fedayeen,* dedicates them to self-sacrifice.

The PLO and its offshoots have as little regard for democratic thinking as for secularism. At the Beirut symposium, for example, a PLO official found the proposed slogan involving democracy strange and distasteful: "Let us face matters honestly. When we speak simply of a Democratic Palestinian State, this means we discard its Arab identity. I say that on this subject we cannot negotiate, even if we possess the political power to authorize this kind of decision, because we thereby disregard a historic truth, namely, that this land and those who dwell upon it belong to a certain environment and a certain region to which we are linked as one nation, one heritage. . . ."

The spokesman for the Democratic Front declared:

This state is not bi-national in the sense that there would be two national states joined together in one form or another. This solution must be rejected, not only because it is inconsistent with our own desire, but also because it is not a true democratic solution. It is rather a solution that will represent the continuation of the national conflict that exists between the Jews and Arabs, not a solution of this conflict. It is impossible to speak of a democratic solution if it is powerless to eliminate the conflict between the different denominations and peoples within the Democratic State. When we speak of democracy it must be clear that we do not mean liberal democracy in the manner of "one man, one vote." We mean a people's democratic regime, which will put an end to the social basis upon which Zionism rests and will consequently settle the class conflicts, and then those among the denominations and peoples.

An Arab state, then, can be "democratic" only if everyone in it is subservient to an Arab majority. The conflict between Jews and Arabs can be solved only by the Arabs remaining Arabs and the Jews becoming something else (or better still, leaving). The PLO and its sponsors do not grant them the right to call themselves a nation, a people or even a cohesive group with the sort of historical ties that entitle the Arabs to yet another state. The Jews are widely characterized, in the deliberations of the terrorist movement, as a "denomination."

The representative of the Iraqi puppet Arab Liberation Front tried to explain why the Kurds, unlike the Jews, are a nationality: "The Kurds comprise a nationality having a distinct, well-known historical, geographical and human dimension. . . ." This, as it happens, did not help the Kurdish minority in Iraq. Moslems but not Arabs, they trace their ancestry through four thousand years with a language and a culture of their own. They number in the hundreds of thousands and have long sought autonomy over the mountainous region which is part of their ancestral home. Today, after years of artillery shelling, napalm and rocket attacks by the armed forces of the Iraqi government, many of their villages stand deserted and desolate, tens of thousands of them are refugees in neighboring Iran, tens of thousands— even Iraqi officials admit—have been uprooted and forcibly resettled in hostile, alien desert land. The Arabs, as they continued the war against another small non-Arab people, could not fail to note that in large measure the Kurds lost their struggle because two trusted big-brothers, Iran and the U.S. together had supplied the required arms, bases and funds, reacted to changing geopolitical facts in the area, and in 1975 abandoned the mountain people as nuisances without value in the new, larger scheme of things.

What would the New Palestine look like? In its earliest stage, according to one line of Arab thinking, it would consist of two salients. Under the plan the Palestinians would take over the landlocked West Bank of Jordan, narrowing Israel just north of Tel Aviv to a mere ten miles in width. They would also occupy the Gaza Strip, which would have a coastline but would not be contiguous with the farmlands of the West Bank. There would be no unity and little economic viability.

A prevalent Arab line called for the state to grow out of lands "wrested from the occupier . . . by any means." Some Arabs saw this occurring by means of war, some through the good offices of the great powers and the UN. (It was expected that Arab pressure, from economic warfare through the stacked arms race to various forms of military action, would provide an assist.) Whichever mechanism would be used, certainly no negotiations with Israel were envisioned. "Negotiations are impossible," the Palestine Corner of Radio Damascus announced in 1974 when its editors heard that the Israeli Knesset was engaging in a purely theoretical discussion as to whether talks with the PLO might ever be conceivable, "not because the Zionists refuse it [sic], but because the Arab nation has never in the past and will never in the future entertain thoughts of negotiating with the Zionist invaders, with the exception of a violent dialogue of war along the borders of confrontation or within the occupied land." Israel's isolation, naturally, would not be broken; there would be no contact between Israel and the bi-partite Arab state and no contact across Israel between the two halves of the new Palestine.

And so the new state would start life with an economic depression of major proportions. On the West Bank alone,

THE USES OF TERROR

45,000 wage earners—7 per cent of the *entire* population—
would lose their jobs in Israel the moment the border
closed. The Gaza Strip, separated from Egypt by the Sinai,
from Lebanon by the Mediterranean, from the West Bank
by a shrunken Israel, would lose not only thousands of jobs
but markets and economic *raison d'être* as well.

And yet, theoretically at least, many thousands would
flock to the new Palestine in response to the revolution's
call. A few might bring money, but more, many more,
would come from the slums of Lebanon and Syria. Housing, jobs, food, schooling, the machinery of distribution, all
would create problems in twin regions with minimal natural
resources, and there could be a surreal re-creation of the
days when the refugees, idle, aimless, huddled in tents and
huts.

That would be the least of it. The new government's
problems would be immensely magnified by the differences
between running a loose federation of revolutionaries and
meeting the imperatives of national unity, human need and
administrative routine. The newcomers would include restless armed men accustomed to settling all problems by violent action, autonomous armed groups loyal to this or that
political philosophy, armed groups allied with this or that
Arab state. Instability, infighting, invitation to civil war and
bloodshed would all be inherent in the situation. In a tiny,
crowded country split by geography, divided by conflicting
ideology and ambitions, beset by economic woes and popu-
lated by old settlers with vested interests and a ragtag horde
of bloodstained veterans of the Lebanese wars, there
would be only one safety valve. It would be in plain sight,
just beyond the dusty plains of Gaza and the hills of the
West Bank.

No Arab leader—with the exception of Syria's President,
Hafez al-Assad, in his deliberate falsehood to *Newsweek*'s

correspondent—has ever said that the struggle against Israel would cease with the establishment of an Arab state in part of Palestine. None has ever said that the mini-state would satisfy Arab appetites and aspirations. Even Sadat tempered his acceptance of the mini-state with the significant words "to start with." And Tunisia, an American favorite because of its muted tones in Arab councils, concurred. In 1974 its foreign minister, Habib Chatti, wrote that the West Bank and Gaza "would not suffice. . . . The Palestinians would need more than these overcrowded bits of territory—and additional land would have to come from Israel and Hussein's Jordan." The noted Egyptian journalist, Mohammed Hassenein Heikal, who speaks for many in the Arab world, has said: "Nobody in Egypt can accept a final peace which leaves a land barrier separating Egypt from the rest of the Arab world to the East. Israel is a barrier which isolates Egypt and prevents movement to the Arabian peninsula, the Gulf and the Levant." By the time such men are finished, Israel will have dwindled to a coastal strip. The PLO crowd and their sponsors have no intentions of leaving even that much.

The PLO's chief observer at the United Nations, Zehdi Labib Terzi, described such a state to a UN committee on Palestine as merely the first step in a two-stage repatriation of all Palestinians. Further, he said in the winter of 1976, all displaced Palestinians had to be "physically in Palestine" and in possession of their abandoned homes and properties before the creation of a "sovereign Palestine state." Terzi went on to point out that this "would alter the demographic balance in Israel to such an extent that it would destroy its Zionist exclusionist character." He called the plan "a prerequisite to peace."

To the neophyte in the Middle East political jungle, this might seem a rather clumsy way of saying that the PLO would accept a small state and adding an offer the Israelis could only refuse. Terzi chose to leave out the rest, which was the work of the Palestine National Council, meeting in Cairo in June, 1974. The Council was the legislative body of the PLO. Its decision-makers, like the PLO membership, represented the wide spectrum of para-military groups which the Arab states recognize as the joint legitimate voice of the nascent Palestine state. Its political decisions were coordinated with the leadership of the Arab states and the Arab League. Due thought had been given to the key decision to be taken at the Cairo meeting, and there had been psychological preparation for the faithful. A month earlier a PLO ideologue, speaking over the Voice of Palestine, said that there were times when a courageous leadership must propose an "interim solution" but that such a proposal would not negate the "historic right" to all of Palestine. The resolution's text was prepared by Yasir Arafat and five other commissioners, among them the fiery George Habash. The resolution spelled out the actual stand of the PLO on a mini-state:

> The PLO will struggle by all possible means, and foremost by means of an armed struggle, for the liberation of the Palestinian lands and the setting up of a patriotic, independent, fighting peoples' regime in every part of the Palestine territory which will be liberated. It affirms that this will only be accomplished through major changes in the balance of forces to the advantage of our people and their struggle.
> The PLO will consider any step toward liberation which is accomplished as a stage in pursuit of its strategy for the establishment of a democratic Palestinian state, as laid down in the decisions of previous National Council meetings.

Salah Khalaf, better known by his *nom de guerre* of Abu Iyad, was one of the more articulate members of the PLO executive committee and a man of driving ambition. In September, 1975, in an interview in Tunisia, he put the sense of that resolution in its proper political context after first pointing to the lesson to be learned from the lost opportunity of 1948:

> . . . If our people . . . had taken possession of the part [of mandated Palestine] to which they were entitled in accordance with the partition plan and had created a state with a view to demanding the remainder of the territory and supporting their demand while being able to rely on their state entity, cadres, *fedayeen* and army, our situation would now be completely different. . . .
> . . . What are we proposing now? We are aware that the creation of a democratic state [in all of Palestine] is a dream which only our sons and future generations will be able to realize. For the time being, we propose the following solution: Every parcel of Palestinian soil which has been evacuated should be placed under the national authority of the Palestinian state . . . every parcel of evacuated soil owes its allegiance to the Palestinian state . . . we would keep it under our control, by force of arms if necessary. . . .

Of course, the goal of a "democratic" state in all of Palestine remained. "A secular state?" asked the interviewer. "Yes, a secular state where everybody would live side by side, including Jews who want to see us dead."

Oddly, the vote for an interim mini-state was quickly followed by an escalation of PLO threats to destroy Israel. Perhaps they felt they must allay the fears of those who might have thought the decision represented capitulation. On July 8, 1974, only a few weeks after the Cairo meeting, Arafat sent a tough cable to a convention of Third World youth in Algiers: "Despite the conspiracies and the cruel, intense provocations which obstructed the march toward liberation . . . , the Palestinian fighters stand fast and are continuing their armed struggle. . . . We are firmly resolved to implement our great goal of liberating our homeland, Palestine, from the clutches of Zionism and founding the democratic Palestinian state over all the territory of Palestine, a state . . . which will be a replacement for the entity created by imperialism, known as Israel."

He wrote to Soviet newspapers to explain that the shift in the line was really tactical: "We have long ago voiced the slogan of establishing an independent democratic state over the entire territory of Palestine. As to the current stage of our struggle . . . , we have decided to create an independent Palestinian rule in every section of the territories after their liberation from the occupiers."

A month later, there was a clarification from Zuheir Muhsin, member of the PLO "Military Department," functionary of the Syrian supported Saiqa: "Israel will not remain in any of its parts, not even in Tel Aviv."

But it was necessary to emphasize and re-emphasize true belief because, what with the smokescreen of peaceful words to the West, even the believers sometimes grew confused. The wrath of Arafat fell upon one Ibrahim Souss, the PLO's man at UNESCO headquarters in Paris, because of a single hopeful statement Souss made about normal contacts between a Palestinian interim state and Israel. Unification, Souss told a *Le Monde* correspondent, "will become inevitable as a realistic outcome" of such contact. The statement was immediately disavowed by the PLO and Souss hastily issued a clarification: "When speaking about the future without borders or barbed wire, I naturally intended a unified democratic state of the total area of Palestine." The clarification did him no good; he was sent back home in disgrace.

Clarification continued. In February, 1976, Arafat displayed the face of moderation to an American Senator, and Abu Iyad had to dispel the resultant erroneous impression that the movement might agree to live with a shrunken Israel. In an interview with the Beirut newspaper *Al Muharrir,* he said: "The PLO has an unquestionable right to set up its national authority on part of Palestinian soil, but that does not at all mean we will settle for a partial state or recognize Israel. On the contrary, we want to recover part of Palestine to try to liberate the rest."

But it was Muhsin, Syria's favorite, who put it all together into a coherent whole, in an interview in December, 1975, with the German weekly, *Die Zeit.* He, for one, was more interested in a clear expression of policy than in conciliatory stances to appease the Western nations:

> We want to live together with them in one country [Muhsin said]. We don't want to throw them into the sea or drive them into the desert.
>
> *Q.* But this actually means denying Israel the right to exist as a state.
>
> *A.* They've got to accept this eventuality. Our right to exist in Palestine takes precedence over theirs.
>
> *Q.* Wouldn't a Palestinian state in the former Jordanian West Bank and Gaza satisfy PLO aims?
>
> *A.* No! Never! We want to get back every bit of land, every field, every village and every house that belonged to us. Nothing will keep us from this! Right is on our side.
>
> *Q.* Do you expect Israel to agree to what is in fact national suicide?
>
> *A.* Israelis must change their way of thinking. They'll see this as the only solution when we force them to their knees—after we've smashed them to pieces militarily!

Such language was buttressed by solemn political theorizing. An al-Fatah monthly wrote: ". . . in a people's war

there is no deterrent inhibition, for its aim is not to defeat
the enemy but to extirpate [*sic*] him . . . destruction of
the enemy is the first and last duty." The cult of death was
fostered by training—the teenaged Lion Cubs tore apart
live chickens as part of their education—and by the aggran-
dizement of terror via the words of the Arab media and
Arab statesmen. In 1969 Yehoshafat Harkabi, the Israeli
student of the terror movement, wrote: "Educating the
present Arab generation in vengeance and brutality, though
it is directed outward, may rebound and take a heavy toll
within the Arab states themselves. The *fedayeen* may well
become a sect. . . . Latent disparities between the *fedayeen* organizations and the Arab states may come into the
open and bring havoc to the Arab societies."

That same year the powers among the Arab states, un-
willing to have lawless armed men wandering in *their* lands
and spreading unrest among *their* people, in effect set Lebanon up for the explosion, forcing that weak and divided
country into a formal agreement giving the *fedayeen* bases,
supply routes and virtual self-government. When the inevitable explosion came in 1975-76, it was a terrible thing.
Tens of thousands, mainly civilians, were killed, a fifth of
the population fled the country. A *New York Times* correspondent wrote: "Christians and Moslems maim the dead,
torture before they kill." *Time* Magazine reported: "Throat
cutting has become the ritual form of execution." Children
died of dehydration a half mile from water. Field guns and
tanks were used at point-blank range in cities. A *Washington Post* correspondent wrote of artillery being fired
"almost anywhere in unthinking anger rather than in any
careful calculation of an army's objectives." A Lebanese
pediatrician concluded that teenagers who had seen the
horror "will go through life believing that the most effective
way to get things done is by force."

In April, 1975, before the conflict broke forth in full fury, Yasir Arafat offered *The Economist* of London his line of sweet reason and said: "We have in the Lebanese experience a significant example that is close to the multi-religious state we are trying to achieve." After succeeding months of horror Atallah Mansour, an Arab and an Israeli, a correspondent for Israel's leading Hebrew daily, a serious man who had spent his adult life trying to interpret one society to the other, asked: "Why should any Israeli believe and trust that the Arab Moslem world is mature enough to accept the Jewish-European state of Israel?"

7

The Spoilers

The Soviet Union has taken part in all stages of the Arab peoples' struggle against aggression and expansionism in the Middle East. . . . This was the case during the difficult days of June, 1967, when criminal aggression was committed against Egypt, Syria and Jordan, with encouragement from the imperialist forces in the West, primarily in the United States. After that war, the Soviet Union helped Egypt and Syria recover their military and economic power. In the last few years it has helped in every possible way to tip the balance of power in favor of the Arabs. Without this it would have been impossible for Egypt and Syria to score their successes of the last war of October, 1973, in the Middle East.

Why did the Soviet Union, which made great efforts to bring about a peaceful political settlement in the Middle East, give—at the same time—modern weapons and modern military equipment to the Arab Republic of Egypt, the Syrian Arab Republic and other Arab countries?

The answer to this question is that the Soviet Union did not oppose the Arabs' use of armed force in the struggle against the aggressors, who persisted in their actions and expansionist plans. This Soviet attitude was repeatedly confirmed in the official statements of Soviet leaders and in many joint Soviet-Arab documents. Naturally, when the last war broke out in October last year as a result of the ill-advised policy of the Israeli rulers, the Soviet Union firmly consolidated its military support for Egypt and Syria, which bore the brunt of the struggle against the aggressor.

These words are not a parody. They were broadcast on Moscow radio on April 14, 1974. Since Moscow radio is a wholly owned subsidiary of the Soviet State, they must be viewed as an accurate reflection of official Kremlin policy. Agit-prop verbiage aside, the statement is an understatement.

It is also revealing, given the June, 1972, meeting in Moscow at which Soviet party chief Leonid Brezhnev and President Richard Nixon laid down "basic principles of relations" between the two countries. The formal agreement pledged the two nations "to do their utmost to avoid military confrontation" and "to do everything in their power so that conflicts or situations will not arise which would serve to increase international tensions."

This was détente, that untranslatable and short-lived retreat from the brink upon which the United States had placed its hopes. A year later Nixon and Brezhnev met again and signed another agreement designed to avert nuclear confrontation. By then the Soviet Union had already violated its first treaty commitment to the United States. Almost immediately after the second agreement was signed, the USSR embarked, through its Arab allies, on a war in the Middle East that raised the specter of superpower confrontation.

In the year between the agreements, the Russians had renewed a generous flow of weapons and specialists to Egypt. They added a new element of ominous sophistication to the region's arsenals by giving Egypt the Scud, a ground-to-ground missile with a 185-mile range and nuclear capability. They showered Syria with weapons—the new T-62 battle tank, MIG-21 fighters, Frog surface-to-surface missiles and, at President Assad's urgent request, a complete in-depth air defense system. They were as considerate in their arms deliveries to Iraq. In short, they made war possible.

In the months immediately following the second solemn superpower agreement, the flow of Soviet weapons turned into a flood. This largesse had one purpose—war. And the timetable of the days leading up to the 1973 war is itself a matter of grim record. On September 22 Sadat summoned the Soviet ambassador and handed him a note to give Brezhnev. The note apparently contained news of the impending attack, and Brezhnev replied promptly. On October 3 the Egyptian President conferred again with the Russian ambassador. On the same day, in Damascus, Assad summoned the Soviet ambassador. Immediately, there was action in Moscow. Huge Antonov-23 transport aircraft were sent to the two capitals and Russian civilian dependents were flown out. Cosmos spy satellites were sent aloft. Soviet vessels sailed out of Port Said and Alexandria. On October 5, a *Pravda* correspondent in Cairo filed this report: "Tension is increasing on the cease-fire line between Syria and Israel. According to assumptions by the Egyptian press, Tel Aviv is preparing a massed attack." The report was wholly fanciful.

The next day, when the Arabs attacked, Moscow sprang into action. There was none of the hesitation and confusion which marked the Kremlin's behavior in June, 1967. Soviet ships with heavy military equipment reached Syria within five days, an impossibility unless the vessels were already loaded and ready to sail when the war began. A massive air-lift was launched within four days of the Yom Kippur attack. In a spectacular show of strength, the USSR massed ninety naval vessels—the greatest number it had ever assembled in the Eastern Mediterranean. The Russians pressured non-confrontation Arab states to support their embattled allies. The response was slower than expected. In his *The Road to Ramadan,* Mohammed Hassenein Heikal recalls a nettled Soviet President Podgorny asking, "What have Iraq and Algeria got all those arms from us for?" On the diplomatic front, the USSR blocked all UN attempts to obtain a cease-fire as long as the Arabs were winning. When the Israelis turned the tide, the Soviet line changed abruptly and the Kremlin moved in complex and threatening ways and brought on a confrontation of frightening proportions with the United States.

During the fighting, as Jim Hoagland of the *Washington Post* revealed three years later, Soviet advisers directed the firing of many of the surface-to-air missiles manned by Syrian crews. This may help explain the fact that in the first days of the fighting the Israeli air losses to SAMs on the Golan front were very high. The veteran journalist also reported that North Korean pilots flew "defensive" combat missions for the Syrians and "evidently worked with Soviet ground controllers, since they did not speak Arabic." Another Soviet ally, Cuba, sent ground troops to Syria and elements of a Cuban brigade were kept in reserve for the final defense of Damascus.

For the Russians, Israel in 1973 was the equivalent of Spain in 1936—a convenient testing ground for arms. The first Frog missiles ever used in war were fired toward an Israeli airfield in Galilee and hit civilian settlements instead. Egypt gave the Scud its baptism by fire, using this impressive weapon against the Israeli bridgehead on the Suez.

Russian air-to-surface Kelts were fired toward Tel Aviv and were dead on target when Israeli aircraft shot them down. The war was a major test for the intricate Russian-made networks of platform-launched SAM missiles and for the miniaturized but murderous SA-7 Grail, fired from the shoulder by a single infantryman. The tank battles of the Golan and the Sinai—the greatest since the World War II duels at Kursk and El Alamein—saw the introduction of the viciously effective Soviet weapon, the wire-guided Sagger anti-tank missile. Indeed, according to one prestigious think tank, the Soviets deliberately failed to warn the U.S. about the coming war in part because they wanted to use the conflict to test weaponry.

Soviet progress after the war was almost as ominous as the blatant Soviet role during the war. The USSR now gathered bases and usage rights of one kind or another in harbors in Algeria, Libya and especially Syria. Russia's missile ships could target every major Sixth Fleet combat vessel, and sea-based Soviet missiles could counter those of the Polaris submarines.

The American public, rushing from reality after the Vietnam trauma, had shut its eyes against the reality of.power in the Mediterranean, but that did not change the facts. In his careful 1976 study, *The Strategic Balance in the Mediterranean,* journalist-diplomat Jesse W. Lewis, Jr., wrote that the Soviet Mediterranean fleet was "a powerful modern naval force with some weapons that are not possessed by the Sixth Fleet." The USSR, he wrote, would soon overcome its one major weakness, lack of sea-based air power, "and thus dramatically alter the psychological balance of power." Lewis painted a frightening picture of the U.S.-USSR naval maneuvers in the near confrontation of October, 1973, saying: "The Soviet commander had his ships in a pre-emptive position and was prepared to open

107

fire." Each of the three American aircraft carriers guarding the Eastern Mediterranean in those grim days, he reported, was dogged by three Soviet warships, one of them a surface-to-surface missile ship, the second a surface-to-air missile ship and the third "probably a tattletale capable of providing mid-course guidance for surface-to-surface missiles fired from another location."

A retired American Vice Admiral, George P. Steele, who had commanded the Seventh Fleet in the Pacific during the final crisis in Vietnam, compared the U.S. and Soviet naval forces in the Mediterranean in the 1973 crisis and concluded flatly that "the Sixth Fleet was staked for sacrifice, deprived of enough sea room for defensive maneuver." Such views are subject to dispute by rival experts, but there is no quarrel about the fact that from 1973 onwards the Soviets have posed major—if not a checkmating—challenge to American naval power in the Mediterranean. Routinely, the Russians maintain there some fifty naval vessels, including missile cruisers, missile-carrying destroyers, submarines and, on occasion, the 15,000-ton helicopter-carrying cruisers *Moskva* and *Leningrad*. As for the lacuna of sea-based air power, naval history was made on July 18, 1976, when the first full-fledged Soviet aircraft carrier, the 40,000-ton *Kiev*, sailed proudly through the Bosporus to join the Soviet Mediterranean flotilla which, at that point, outnumbered the U.S. Sixth Fleet by a dozen ships. Two other *Kiev*-class carriers were under construction. The days when the Soviet navy was a token force, virtually ignored by the Kremlin and taken lightly by the West, were gone.

Russia also maintained a significant presence on the eastern edge of the Arabian land mass, along the route Western supertankers ply to Europe and Japan. The Soviet Union was building a base for Iraq at Umm Qasr at the head of the

Persian Gulf. The USSR had naval and air facilities on the strategic South Yemen island of Socotra, military installations in Aden, major facilities at Berbera on the Somalia coast and privileges at harbors scattered across the Indian Ocean. In a world-wide naval exercise in 1975, the second of its kind in five years, Soviet aircraft flying from Berbera as well as from air bases in Russia provided support for naval units in the Mediterranean, the Black Sea, the Arabian Sea and the Indian Ocean.

All this represented a tremendous change in a single generation. Twenty years before the Yom Kippur War, the Soviet Union did not have even a slender toehold in the Middle East. The subsequent Russian rise to major stature in the region was based on a willingness to exploit the Arab hatred for Israel without shame or constraint.

The relationship between the Arabs and the Russians is thoroughly amoral. The Russians could not care less what happens to Israel. The Arabs, by and large, do not share Soviet strategic goals. Soviet ideologues have contempt for Arab bourgeois nationalism. The Arabs, deeply Islamic, clan-oriented, conservative socially and culturally, generally detest Soviet ideology. The Nazi pilots who tested bombing tactics against Guernica at least were politically sympathetic to Franco fascism; the Russian experts on the Suez and in the Golan were involved in a cause which did not move them, except for occasional upswellings of old-fashioned, Russian anti-Semitism. For years, Egypt has been throwing local communists into jail, and lately Syria has been moving from state planning to free-market capitalism; the Russians are not bothered by such contradictions. The USSR, for a complex of reasons of its own, permits a controlled flow of Russian Jews to migrate to Israel; the Arabs close their eyes to this moral sabotage of their case.

There was a happy symbiosis here. The Arabs exploit the Soviet Union so they can wage war on Israel. The USSR makes use of the Arabs to wage war on the West.

The Soviet goals were self-evident—raw power, the erosion of the West, at least partial control over Arab oil. As of now, the Kremlin does not need the oil, but is acutely aware that Western Europe relies on the Arabs for 70 per cent of its oil and that Japan imports more than 90 per cent of its energy needs. Long before the October, 1973, crisis, Moscow was boldly encouraging the Arabs to use the oil weapon; when oil was used to blackjack the West, Moscow radio made no effort to conceal its glee; when the Arabs showed signs of readiness to abandon the embargo, Moscow urged them to remain firm. It was all part of the same war.

Yasir Arafat, in political and socio-economic terms, is a reactionary. Some of his best friends were the Saudi feudalists. (His eventual alliance with "leftist" Moslem forces in the war in Lebanon was based on tactical needs and a shared hate, not ideology.) Arafat had not the slightest desire to revolutionize society. Yet he was heartily supported by the Russians. His al-Fatah was Soviet-armed. His men carried the Middle East's most popular killer instrument, the Kalashnikov automatic rifle. Arab terrorists working in the West even had access to the Soviet-made shoulder-held SA-7 anti-aircraft missile; one group was seized by Italian police outside the Rome airport while aiming an SA-7 at a passenger-laden aircraft. Al-Fatah men have been trained in the Soviet Union and its satellites, and a Communist agency apparently gave operational information to the terrorist hijackers of a train carrying Russian-Jewish emigrants from the Czech border to Vienna.

In accepting the PLO, the Kremlin chose pragmatism and

opportunism over its own natural psychological tendencies. The Soviet Union has always distrusted terrorists as asocial and uncontrollable. When, however, al-Fatah and the others began gaining popularity in the Arab world, the Soviet press quickly recognized the Palestinian Revolution and labeled the gunmen "partisans," a term of great praise in the Soviet lexicon. (To this day, however, Soviet journalism tried mightily to ignore or play down the more embarrassing terrorist exploits and to emphasize instead the immorality of Israeli retaliation. Sometimes terrorist excesses forced the Kremlin through complex mental gymnastics. In reacting to the atrocity at the Munich Olympics, *Pravda* said: "Arab reactionaries and Israeli agents are deliberately pushing the Palestinians toward extremism in order to create in the international public the idea that the Arab partisans are only fanatical terrorists. . . . Reactionary circles are trying to use the events at the Olympic Games as a pretext for intensifying military provocations against the Arab countries.") In time, the Palestinian cause became a sanctified war of national liberation and the PLO gained *de facto* recognition and honor in Moscow. The cost was modest and seemed well worthwhile, but complications inevitably arose and they were partly Moscow's fault. By welcoming Arafat and friends to Moscow, by repeatedly blessing the movement on the radio waves, by supplying arms to the terrorists directly rather than through allied Arab states, the Kremlin helped the PLO delude itself into the belief that it was not simply an Arab League tool but had an independent existence. That delusion in turn helped lead to the war in Lebanon. It was a war which baffled the hard-headed Russians—for did it not divert Arab energies from the struggle with Israel?—and for a time they zigzagged on policy, in the process losing face in Damascus. There could, how-

111

ever, be long-term benefits; the traumatic war was bound to
result in new shock waves in Araby, new unstable situations welcome to Moscow.

Amorality encourages deception. The façade of detente
was merely part of the deception of 1972–73. The scenario
also included a dramatic "split" between Moscow and Cairo. A month after Nixon, Brezhnev and Kissinger made
headlines and what is termed history at the June, 1972,
Moscow summit meeting, Sadat dramatically expelled hundreds of Soviet experts from Egypt. The West, always eager to exaggerate Soviet "setbacks," was gleeful. Here was
evidence that the Soviet flow of arms would dry up. Here
was proof of permanent estrangement.

The West was wrong. After the war the Egyptians were
unable to resist the human temptation to boast—to their
Arab brethren, never to the outside world—of the success
of what they themselves called a "deception campaign." In
October, 1974, the authoritative Cairo weekly *Ros el-Youssef* published an account of Sadat's "brilliant plan of political camouflage" during the period leading up to the Yom
Kippur attack:

> The various [Egyptian] government agencies spread ru-
> mors and stories that were exaggerated, to say the least,
> about deficiencies, both quantitative and qualitative, [in
> weaponry] . . . required to begin the battle against Israel,
> at the very time when . . . Egypt and the USSR had
> reached agreement [on arms supplies covering the latter half
> of 1973]. Moreover, the Egyptian press frequently gave
> prominence to an inclination [in Cairo] to seek arms in the
> West. . . . All this talk about armaments and their short-
> ages was intended to create the impression . . . that one of
> the reasons why Egypt was incapable of starting war was
> the absence of high-quality weapons. . . . And the whole
> world was taken by surprise when zero hour arrived. . . .

The episode of July, 1972 . . . was exploited and many intentionally or unintentionally failed to hear the words of President Sadat and his repeated emphasis that this episode was no more than "an interlude with our friend," as always happens among friends . . . these Soviet experts had fulfilled an important task in connection with the network of missiles and other delicate weapons [i.e., and having fulfilled the task, could leave]. The Egyptian deception campaign, moreover, was able to reap considerable benefit from this episode . . . because it raised questions about the genuineness of the regime's threats to resort to war; after all, how would the Egyptian army be able to fight without the presence of thousands of Russian experts . . . ?

And when the war started in fact, there was the additional surprise that unlimited Soviet support was extended both in the international arena and in the area of military equipment. The . . . Pentagon spokesman, on the morrow of the battle, expressed his opinion about this surprise: "We never imagined that the Soviet Union would do what it has done, after the tough verbal campaign against it in the Arab world, and after the cooling of relations with Cairo following the exodus of the Soviets."

The account in the Cairo weekly was not the careless jottings of a sensation-seeking journalist on a dull news day. Its publication was timed for the war's first anniversary; *Ros el-Youssef* is the official organ of the Arab Socialist Union, Sadat's party, Egypt's only party; the paper reported, without official contradiction, that the author of the account, a military affairs' correspondent, had been permitted to see secret material and that Sadat himself had provided assistance. A year later, Sadat confirmed the basic point of it all, telling an interviewer for Cairo radio that the ouster of the Soviet experts had been "a strategic cover" and "a splendid strategic distraction."

In cases such as this, it takes two to practice deception. No student of Soviet affairs doubts any longer that the Kremlin was as much a part of the deception as the Egyptian leadership itself. The Kremlin pretended to have been insulted after the "expulsion," but was able to contain the insult so wondrously well that Soviet arms shipments over the next fourteen months included hundreds of tanks, among them an improved model of the mighty T-62, and amounted to hundreds of millions of dollars worth of equipment. The Soviets were also obliging enough to leave dozens of MIG-21s behind when their experts left Cairo in alleged disgrace. Some of those very experts went directly to Syria and, by amazing timing, were on hand to serve usefully in the 1973 war. A Sadat associate later wrote that Egypt had approved this transfer "because the national interests required the continued existence of Soviet experts in the region."

The lesson was wasted on the West. After the war, for the most pragmatic of reasons, Egypt turned to Washington rather than Moscow in its efforts to gain diplomatically what could not be achieved on the battleground. Forgetting past precedent, Western commentators rushed to conclude that the friendship was dead. The death was exaggerated. Differences and tensions did, in fact, arise, but Moscow was most patient with Cairo. The flow of arms was sharply cut back only after Egypt's 1973 losses had been replaced and after shipments, including hundreds of tanks, dozens of aircraft, new items representing an escalation in the qualitative arms race, reached perhaps a billion dollars or more. (Soviet pricing in weaponry is often arbitrary, a matter of the State's convenience rather than of cost accounting.) Despite well-publicized slights and the exchange of cold words, Moscow and Cairo signed a fat new trade agreement and there were friendly high-level discussions.

Who was to say that the new "split" was not "an interlude with our friend"?

Russia does not insult easily. The Soviet Union has been a superpower long enough to know that clients can be difficult, even contradictory, even fickle, that associates will sometimes do their own thing almost in defiance of the patron state, that smaller friends can and—particularly in the infuriating Middle East—often do have clashing goals. Moscow remained calm. It saw no reason for permanent destruction of valuable relationships; fickle old clients may return to the fold in time. Meanwhile, Moscow had continued opportunities to play its games in the area. If Cairo grew cool temporarily, Damascus could be warmed; if Damascus became difficult, there was Iraq, the PLO, Libya, and others. What was important was to retain momentum and bases in the area. The long-range war was more significant than individual skirmishes.

For the Russians, the war went on. They continued to pour weapons into Syria and other "progressive" states. They managed to deal with Libya's Qaddafi, despite his Islamic fanaticism, and they have contracted to build him a nuclear reactor and to supply a cornucopia of arms. They are constructing a major base at Latakia on the Syrian coast. They are prominent in the diplomatic struggle for maximalist Arab demands, earning favor with Arabs everywhere. They have the Arab allies to frustrate any significant settlement.

In one sense, neither the Russians nor the Americans have changed the Middle East. It remains, as it was with the arrival of the Americans in the 1940s and the Russians in the 1950s, an area of unstable governments, deep social unrest, political injustice and economic inequality. If instability can be measured scientifically, the region is probably more chaotic, more dangerous than before the powers blessed it with their presence. The Middle East remains united in hatred of Israel, disunited in every other way. Despite all the maddening frustrations and insane complications, it remains a fertile playground for Russia, so adept at the spoiler's game. Whatever happens, the Russians have room to maneuver. True, shuttle diplomacy did give the United States the spotlight temporarily, but it solved nothing and led to bitter inter-Arab disputes which Moscow could seek to exploit. A Geneva "peace" conference could present the Kremlin with opportunities to support the most extreme Arab position. The continuation of a situation that is neither war nor peace between Arab and Israeli means continued chances to foment trouble. An Arab state in part of Palestine means opportunity to promote irredentism and its creation would be an invitation to Moscow to form yet another client-patron relationship. An Arab state in all of Palestine would solve no Middle Eastern problems but would free the Arabs, to Russia's satisfaction, to devote themselves full-time to their internal wars and power struggles.

"The question," the veteran Israeli leader Yigal Allon said in 1971, "is sometimes asked: 'Does the Soviet Union desire the destruction of Israel?' My answer would be: 'No, but she might not do anything to prevent it.'" In view of what has happened since then, that was probably both too kind and too simple a reply to a disturbing question.

8

The Well as Big
as the Ritz

When oil men talk prices, they generally use "Arabian light crude f.o.b. Ras Tanura" as their yardstick. Its recent history is instructive. In December, 1965, it was selling for $1.80 a barrel. Five years later, it was still $1.80 a barrel. Six months after that, in June, 1971, the price rose to $2.21 a barrel. In January, 1972, it was $2.48; in January, 1973, $2.59; in October, 1973, $5.12; in January, 1974, $11.65 a barrel.

These sets of figures, awful or wonderful, depending upon whether you are buying or selling, represent a veritable revolution—the oil-pricing revolution. The Arabs have encouraged the world to believe that it is related to a terribly poignant Arab quest for reversal of Israeli injustice and aggression. This is in no way true.

Economists, banking houses, journalists, senatorial committeemen, international analysts and military experts have studied the price of oil and produced works laden with statistics and details. They agree that the causes of the mad rise lie outside the Arab-Israel conflict.

117

Seven American economists, four of them Nobel Prize winners, concurred as the oil crisis raged in late 1973. Among them were John Kenneth Galbraith of Harvard, Paul Samuelson and Kenneth Arrow of MIT. Their statement said:

> There was and is no connection between Middle East peace and the oil monopoly of Arab and non-Arab nations. If some perfect Middle East political settlement were reached tomorrow, the OPEC countries would not give up a cent of their gains, and they would not cease to consider when and how much to raise prices. To suggest a connection between Arab-Israel strife and the contrived scarcity of oil to drive up prices is to commit a *non sequitur.*

The Senate Foreign Relations Subcommittee on Multinational Corporations, headed by Frank Church (D-Idaho), labored for months on what has to be considered the definitive study of the oil revolution. Its careful report stated:

> It would be unrealistic to believe that a Middle East peace settlement would automatically lead to lower oil prices. The leadership within OPEC in raising prices has come from Iran and Venezuela, countries which have a minimal interest in the Arab-Israel dispute. . . . The October War . . . accentuated but did not initiate a process of price acceleration; that process was well advanced before the War began.

Edith Penrose, professor of economics at the School of Oriental and African Studies, University of London, is one of the world's experts on Middle East oil and the business and diplomatic machinations surrounding that commodity. In the *Journal of the American Academy of Arts and Sciences* she wrote: "The October, 1973, increases in posted oil prices were not related to the war."

118

The Arabs would have us think otherwise. They have said so with such regularity that the skyrocketing price of oil is forever linked in the consciousness of the West with the Arab oil embargo of the Yom Kippur War. The fantastic increase in oil prices is actually an outgrowth of an alliance formed more than a decade earlier by the oil-producing countries of the Persian Gulf plus Venezuela. This was OPEC, the Organization of Petroleum Exporting Countries, and its goal was to control and manipulate the price of oil. Its main stumbling block were the so-called Seven Sisters, seven multinational corporations operating in concert to control the market to their own advantage. The Seven Sisters had an ally in the U.S. government, which obligingly interpreted the tax laws to enable them to amass enormous profits and, with the money, great political leverage. Such giants as Mobil, Exxon, Gulf and Texaco are to be challenged only by the very powerful. Power is an elusive and contrary prize. OPEC's membership grew until the organization represented enormous potential power, but its constituent countries were too weak to grasp at power. Until a leader came along who was willing to risk a blackball from the massed oil companies, the oil-producing countries had no voice at all in the prices and marketing of their fabulous resource.

It was Qaddafi of Libya, that unstable visionary, who finally took the risk. His revolution was only a year old when he challenged the system in 1970. Choosing to avoid a confrontation with the colossi among the oil companies, he selected as his target a weaker "independent," Occidental of California. Occidental capitulated to Libya's demands and agreed, to the consternation of the other oil companies, to a significant increase in prices and "taxes," or oil royalties.

A professor of economics at Amherst later said: "The decline of the West began in Libya with Occidental." Time may yet prove him right. After Occidental, Exxon capitulated in Libya and the other "majors" followed. They preferred a short-sighted squabble with the independents to a showdown with the Arabs, and the State Department preferred appeasement of the Arabs to an undignified quarrel over prices. Price inflation spread across the oil world. Within months there was a general agreement, signed in Teheran, which raised prices in the Persian Gulf for the first time in thirteen years. The accord was linked to an inflation index. It was supposed to ensure five stable years for the industry. It did nothing of the sort.

What followed has been tied to a singular lack of direction on the part of the United States government. Later, the Federal Energy Office was to commission an expert report on the oil situation; the report concluded that "Libya's success demonstrated to all producers that they could impose unilateral changes upon the companies without being challenged by consumer governments, particularly the United States." By then, failure of the U.S. to act had become nothing short of a calamity.

Since there was no profit in absorbing the enormous hike in the price of Arabian crude and its Venezuelan equivalent, the Seven Sisters and their colleague companies passed the increase on to the American consumer. They were able to do so because the West and Japan had become critically dependent on imported oil during the preceding decade. Gone were the good old days when the U.S. mined and refined practically all of its own fuel, and Europe and Japan benefited from the resultant cheapness of Middle East oil. The industrial capacity of the U.S. and its allies was on the line. It was a seller's market and, to understate the matter, the oil companies took their profits and put into the hands of such merciful beings as the Shah of Iran and King Feisal of Saudi Arabia, power over the economic well-being of a good part of the world. And the U.S. government let it happen.

". . . The governing assumption of U.S. policy," the Church Committee report said of the period leading up to the 1973 oil revolution, "was that the U.S. national interest and the companies' interests were convergent and not divergent. . . . There was no strategic overview of the possible disastrous political and economic implications of an absence of spare productive capacity geographically located outside of the OPEC area. . . . The U.S. government had no energy policy and no institutional capacity to formulate one. International oil questions were the exclusive purview of the companies and a select group of State Department officials."

It is a dogma in the United States that its government is independent of any ties but those large involvements with the general welfare referred to in the Bill of Rights. The State Department is usually viewed as a staging ground from which idealistic young persons graduate to imposing embassies in the fullness of their years. These persons spend many decades in the service of their country and they are not swayed by associations, no matter how deep or long-standing, with the business world. The "select group of State Department officials" referred to in the Church Committee report would be, in those terms, as free of bias in the matter as beings from outer space. The expertise which qualified them to deal with international oil questions would have been acquired without prejudice and stored in some inviolate sector of the mind. Therefore, the discovery that a combine of U.S. oil companies had given OPEC free reign over an economy which virtually runs on oil might have been expected to have an effect in the State Department roughly comparable to that of the San Andreas Fault on California. How, then, can we explain the complacent acceptance of the events that were, in time, to lead to a six-fold increase in oil prices?

Oil states like Bahrein, Kuwait and Saudi Arabia are hard training grounds for eager young State Department personnel. Their climates are unspeakable. Their women are out of bounds. They ban liquor and they aren't particularly fond of foreigners, especially infidel foreigners. There is a degree of commingling between the natives of these harsh and difficult sheikhdoms and American officials, but there is genuine surcease to be had in the villas and the clubs of the oil companies. A friendship forged in an alien environment has depth and dimension and, often, a very long life. This helps to explain the tendency of certain middle-aged, middle-level State Department officials to take early retirement and become executives of oil companies. It may also tell us something about that "governing assumption of U.S. policy" which could not differentiate between the interests of a group of greedy, gigantic oil companies and the national interests of the United States of America.

In the spring of 1973, none other than King Feisal of Saudi Arabia decided to use this bond of cronyism to his advantage. He had a word with the representatives of the oil companies who had drilling rights in his country. Feisal wanted a change in U.S. policy toward Israel and, he let it be known that he was prepared to get rough with the oil companies if he did not get his way. From that moment on, there was a burst of activity in oil circles, which had barely stirred when the price of oil began its terrifying upward spiral. Mobil paid for advertisements warning the American public of the dangers of offending the Saudis, while the board chairman of Standard of California sent a letter to all its stockholders saying there "must be . . . more positive support" for the Arab effort for peace in the Middle East. By October, when the Arab armies struck at Israel, there

THE WELL AS BIG AS THE RITZ

was some high-level intervention by some influential people.

One of these was John J. McCloy, a partner in the New York law firm of Milbank, Tweed, Hadley and McCloy. He was what is sometimes called a Very Senior Man; he had been U.S. High Commissioner for Germany, chairman of the Chase Manhattan Bank, an assistant secretary of war, president of the World Bank, chairman of the Ford Foundation, and adviser to Presidents. He was the lawyer for 23 oil companies and four of these were giants with Saudi Arabian oil rights, the great consortium known as Aramco. A week after the outbreak of the Yom Kippur War, McCloy sent a memo by messenger to the White House addressed to President Nixon himself. The memo informed the President that Saudi Arabia was poised to embargo oil if the U.S. continued to support Israel. It was signed by the chairmen of the four Aramco companies and it was accompanied by a covering letter from McCloy.

Senator Church, whose subcommittee delved deep into such matters, had more to say about the incident:

"The letter appeared on its face to be from the American companies. The presidents signed, the Aramco owners— but it was in fact the work of the Saudi Arabian government. And . . . after they had sent the letter, they reported back to Saudi Arabia that they had done as they'd been told, that they had followed instructions."

On October 16, ten days after the Aramco warning to the White House, the OPEC countries (including Venezuela and Iran) raised the price of oil a full 70 per cent without any prior discussion with the oil companies. In any other month of any other year, the West might have reacted sharply not only to the enormity of the price rise but also to its ominous implications. A day later, however, the Arabs, led by Feisal, embargoed oil, and there was such panic in

123

the client countries that both the question of the unilateral action and the price increases dropped abruptly into limbo.

There were no coincidences here. The veteran diplomatic correspondent Tad Szulc later wrote that the Arabs had "used the October war as an excuse to quadruple their prices." An obvious linkage existed between the price increase and the embargo a day later.

For the West, the moment for action was irretrievably lost. When, barely two months later, OPEC met again at the urging of the Shah of Iran and raised oil prices by another 130 per cent, nobody was in any shape to bargain.

The oil states, enjoying their monopolistic status, were now charging more than $11 a barrel for oil which, *The Economist* of London noted, "costs ten cents a barrel to produce in much of the Middle East and whose marginal operating costs (once rigs are in place. . .) are sometimes barely over two cents a barrel." But the oil companies saw no particular reason to bargain. They had, once again, passed the price increases on to the consumer. At a Senate hearing later, Aramco's senior vice president was repeatedly asked what incentive the company and its American partners had to press for lower prices. He could not think of any.

On the embargo, Aramco did its duty—by Saudi Arabia. The Church committee discovered that the Saudis, lacking the skills to administer the embargo properly, relied on Aramco and its American owners. Company compliance was so complete, Church said, that it included "the operation of a primary and secondary embargo aimed at the U.S. military."

From the new American ambassador in Riyadh there was bold initiative in the wrong direction. James Akins had been director of the Office of Fuels and Energy at the State Department, part of the "select group" of officials referred to by the Church committee report, and he knew everybody in oil. Now he met with American oil company officials in his air-conditioned embassy and gave them some fascinating and detailed advice.

Akins' advice was immediately circulated to the proper parties in the U.S., the executives of the four Aramco partners. The cable that went out to them from colleagues in Saudi Arabia urged them to make use of influential friends to the fullest. Leaders of the industry, the cable said, were "to use their contacts at highest levels of USG [the insiders' acronym for the U.S. Government] to hammer home point that oil restrictions are not going to be lifted unless political struggle is settled in manner satisfactory to Arabs. Akins also felt industry leaders should be careful to deliver message in clear unequivocal way so there could be no mistake about industry position. It seems that some communications problems between industry and USG have existed in past which Akins feels are attributable in part to industry presentation not being direct and to the point. . . ."

Since then, industry presentation has indeed been direct and to the point. The oil companies have creatively aided the Arabs to spread the message that the Israelis are responsible for the embargo and the high price of oil. The link they have forged between Israel and the oil crisis has lent widespread credence to the spurious belief that oil prices would come down if the United States were to aid the Arab states in their war against Israel. Even as Saudi Arabia proceeded with nationalization of Aramco, the oil companies cleaved to their slavish line of appeasement in exchange for continued marketing rights to Saudi oil. As the takeover neared completion, Achmed Zaki Yamani, the Saudi oil minister, traveled to Washington and rubbed a few noses in the mess they had made of the economy. There would be compensation for the Aramco companies, he said, and no rise was contemplated in the price of oil—that year.

Yamani could talk that way in Washington because the

Arabs of the Persian Gulf had, meanwhile, become the richest people in the world. The actual embargo on oil had lasted scarcely six months. It had not achieved its ostensible purpose—the United States had, finally, supported Israel. But it had made its point, which was to prove that the Arabs were willing to rend and tear their allies to get what they wanted. It had ended, however, while the revolution set in motion by OPEC had scarcely begun. By March, 1976, when Achmed Zaki Yamani promised that for the next nine months the price of oil would not rise above its current, though exorbitant, level, there had been a monumental money shift from the oil-consuming countries to the oil producers of the Middle East. It was probably the greatest transfer of wealth in modern history.

It was so massive, so tremendous in its potential, that no one was able to fathom it, to measure it or to assess its impact. OPEC's cash intake had risen in four years from $8 billion a year to $100 billion annually—as the direct result of oil sales—but there were no estimates of income from the investments this vast increase made possible. Experts fell back on mind-boggling projections. The U.S. Treasury thought that, by 1985, OPEC countries would be importing goods and services at the rate of $133 billion a year. The World Bank concluded that, by 1985, OPEC's surplus would reach $1.2 trillion. That is a sum equal to the total U.S. gross national product in a good year. It is more than double the total value—between $500 and $600 billion at 1976 prices—of all the companies listed on the New York Stock Exchange; a hundred years or more, an investment banker pointed out, had been required to accumulate the productive capacity represented by those listed firms.

In the here and now, the figures are no less startling. It is not going to happen, but if the sheikhs of the Arab Emirates should ever decide to share their oil revenue equally with their ragged subjects, there would be $35,000 a year for every man, woman and child in each of the underdeveloped little fiefdoms.

What do they do with it all? On a personal level, they squander it with varying degrees of disregard for good taste. One sheikh rampaged through Harrods of London at Christmas-time and spent nearly $150 thousand in a single afternoon; the plush department store remained open an extra seventy-five minutes so he could finish shopping at leisure. Millions of dollars of the world's oil revenues have been lost at the tables in Europe's casinos; one oil sheikh dropped $6 million in a single evening at Monte Carlo. It is commonplace for a visiting Arab to take a whole floor of a Paris hotel for an entourage that can, within the hour, be supplemented by a sizable group of high-priced call girls. The private clinics of Europe have now set aside their most expensive suites for Arabs—two such clinics in London displayed "No Parking" signs in English and Arabic—and travelers between Zurich and London have begun to call Swissair "SwissArab." Saudi Arabia was now sponsoring education through university level, but the daughter of Sheikh Yamani stood out at sober Bryn Mawr as much for her false eyelashes, diamond earrings and couturier clothes as for the constant presence of her security guard. Gulf sheikhs, all of whom had mansions at home, were responsible for nearly half the housing purchases in the better sections of London in 1975, a year when, according to the *Observer* of London, Arabs bought an astonishing 75,000 British houses, including such trifles as Mereworth Castle and the one-time home of Clive of India in Berkeley Square. Real estate agents were unable to find enough property in the $200,000-plus range to satisfy their Arab clients, the respected British weekly said, reporting that one oil sheikh bypassed the agents, landed his helicopter on an estate in the Thames Valley and stepped out in his resplendent white robes to make "a substantial offer" for the property.

As nations, the Arabs are buying billions in goods, from food-processing plants to trucks and even to power generators, from the U.S., Britain, France, Japan, Italy, West Germany, Holland and others. The number of Westerners busy putting together the complex new installations is rising geometrically. To Westerners with eyes to see, it is obvious that the power to buy goods and to rent people can be used as well for geopolitical blackmail.

Vast Arab sums arc being invested abroad. In 1974, according to the U.S. Treasury, the OPEC nations transferred $11 billion—18 per cent of their oil profits—to the United States. At that rate, they would achieve in slightly more than nine years what the U.S., at the height of its economic power after World War II, had required 25 years to accomplish—the investment of $100 billion overseas. The Treasury Department also estimated that, during the first nine months of 1975, 75 per cent of all foreign portfolio investment in the U.S. came from OPEC sources. A Senate Banking Committee report warned: "Such investment could constitute a powerful economic weapon should the Arab states attempt to employ it to achieve political ends."

It all seemed the more ominous because a large part of these billions was invested directly by Arab governments. An Assistant Secretary of the Treasury had to agree with Senator Church that "we are faced with a new type of foreign investment, that is, of central governments who wish to invest surplus revenues." The problem was thus neatly defined, but no one did anything about it.

The problem was rendered all the more grim by the fact that most of the world seemed unable to gather the moral strength to oppose Arab blackmail when applied. The

Arabs' vast new wealth was proving a wondrously effective weapon in depriving Israel of markets and sources of supply. When the Arabs used the oil weapon during the 1973 crisis, Western Europe yielded almost immediately and mouthed the words which the Arabs wanted mouthed. Japan, that fierce defender of freedom of trade, quickly followed suit, breaking with American policy for the first time since 1945; Japan's Prime Minister later explained to the U.S. Secretary of State—according to the well-informed Israeli journalist Matti Golan in his *Secret Conversations of Henry Kissinger*—that he had no Jewish voters to worry about. In Black Africa, where an effective—because realistically modest—technical aid program had won Israel many friends, nation after nation obeyed the Arabs and broke relations with Israel. In the midst of the oil crisis, Kenya's tough old President Jomo Kenyatta told his people that "we should not poke our noses into . . . the conflicts of other peoples" but would ·"remain friends of all and enemies of none." Ten days later Kenya recanted and severed its supposedly strong ties with Israel. It all added up to a lesson in the exercise of raw power which the Arabs would not quickly forget. (Three years later Kenyatta was able to regain a portion of his national pride and simultaneously humiliate his infuriating, half-mad neighbor, Idi Amin of Uganda. When daring Israelis rescued the threatened Jewish passengers of an Air France plane hijacked to Uganda by Arab terrorists and their fanatical German allies, Kenya permitted the rescue planes to refuel at Nairobi airport en route home. Given Arab economic and political clout, however, restoration of Kenyan-Israeli diplomatic relations was beyond Kenyatta's power.)

Meanwhile, the Saudis, whose development budget had been operating at an eight-figure deficit only a few years earlier, were investing vast sums in world money markets. By 1976, SAMA, the Saudi Arabian Monetary Agency, reportedly held a breathtaking $21 billion in short-term deposits in banks across the Western world. The Saudi government poured investments into the United States and by 1976 held more than $6 billion in short-term assets—bank deposits and treasury bills—in the U.S. Saudi holdings in U.S. government bonds, minuscule in the early 1970s, jumped from $2 billion in 1975 to $6 billion a year later. The Saudis entered the stock market cautiously, with an initial investment of $200 million in Wall Street, but by 1976 official Saudi holdings in corporate stocks and bonds were up to $1.5 billion. The Saudis also invested heavily in Japanese industrial bonds. This left them with great sums still untapped; according to the International Monetary Fund, Saudi Arabia had reached a status where it was second only to the industrial power of West Germany in size of gold and foreign currency holdings—$23.7 billion vs. $38.1 billion.

Kuwait became the fifth largest investor in World Bank bonds. Kuwait also bought into a cross-section of American industry—Avon Products, General Motors, General Electric, Eastman Kodak, IBM, Minnesota Mining and Manufacturing, National Cash Register. A group of Kuwaitis paid $27 million for a property on the Champs Elysées in Paris. The Kuwait Investment Company, owned 50-50 by the government and private investors, bought the island of Kiawah off the South Carolina coast for $17.4 million in cash. The firm proceeded to make plans for a $100 million residential resort and, simultaneously, put up $10 million to begin work on a hotel and shopping mall in downtown Atlanta.

Abu Dhabi spent a week's oil revenue to buy, again for cash, a 44 per cent interest in an insurance company building in London. Arab interests are involved in multi-million dollar deals in Brazil. New-rich Arabs have bought two banks in a small California town with combined assets of $140 million. Some of the new Arab money-men are making impressive individual investments; one is said to have purchased a million shares—at $9 a share—in Occidental Oil, an act which might have had a touch of irony in it.

Millions of dollars, tens of millions, hundreds of millions, billions—no one knows how much—are being covertly transferred from one country to another, from the Persian (or Arab) Gulf to Europe to the U.S. and, perhaps, back or part way back again. Major investments are being made with laundered oil money. It is conveniently anonymous. One of New York's wisest investment bankers, Felix Rohatyn, alerted the Church Committee to the problem of disclosure, to the question of "who the ultimate buyer actually is. . . . You will have governments that will be financing third parties . . . you will have money coming in from foreign banks without identification of the ultimate owner . . . it is very, very difficult to identify money because the ability of the human brain to create defenses and subterfuges is very great. . . . It is very possible we will have great difficulty knowing who owns us. . . ." The Senate Banking Committee was disturbed by the problem as well, pointing to the "widespread use" of "nominee" or "street names" to register stock holdings, noting with distaste that, at one point in 1973, 25 of the 30 largest shareholders of Mobil Oil and 28 of the 30 largest shareholders of Ford Motor were "nominees." That sort of thing "poses serious obstacles to determining who owns and controls American corporations," the committee said, and it was clearly thinking about the potential of the Arab threat.

(The Arabs used some of their money to hire the right talent in the right places. "During the past several years," *Parade Magazine* reported in mid-1976, "the Arabs have spent far more money than any other interest group to support the activities of foreign agents in this country." The Arabs, according to the weekly, outspent the French and British who had been lavish in their campaign to win landing rights for the supersonic Concorde. In Washington, where it is always important to have access to men of influence and power, Algeria reportedly paid former Defense Secretary Clark Clifford's law firm an annual retainer of $150,000, and former Attorney General Richard Kleindienst $120,000 annually. The Saudis were paying $100,000 a year to Frederick G. Dutton, a former adviser to the late Sen. Robert F. Kennedy. J. William Fulbright, a sharp critic of Israel during his long tenure as chairman of the Senate Foreign Relations Committee, won business from the United Arab Emirates when he joined a prestigious Washington law firm after defeat at the polls. Private corporations also had an appreciative eye for Americans with experience and contacts in government. The Triad group, part of a many-chambered, $400 million financial empire built by a Saudi entrepreneur, was able to hire a former Assistant Secretary of State for Economic Affairs, no less, as a consultant. The Saudi businessman, it happened, was a good friend of the Saudi Defense Minister, a major arms supplier to the Arab world, a free-wheeling and controversial figure linked to some fancy deals, allegedly involved in six-figure payoffs and, incidentally, a defender of the Arab boycott against Israel.)

Many Arab millions are held in the form of short-term deposits in the major money markets. In 1974, the largest single depositor in New York's First National City Bank (Citibank), the nation's second largest banking chain, was none other than the Government of Kuwait. Kuwait had deposits totaling $1.7 billion—or $1 for every $25 deposited in the bank. Citibank seemed to feel that it could replace any sudden withdrawal even of that amount of money, though it might have to pay higher interest rates to attract substitute monies quickly, but federal bank examiners were concerned about the "leverage" Kuwait was gaining.

A later survey by the Federal Reserve Board showed that the Arab oil states had no less than $11.25 billion in deposits in the nation's six largest banks. In addition to Citibank, these banking powers were Bank of America, Chase Manhattan, Morgan Guaranty, Manufacturers Hanover and Chemical. Huge though these banks were, the Arab deposits amounted to more than 5 per cent of their overall deposits.

The Federal Reserve Board would go no further. It refused to provide a country-by-country breakdown despite the urgings of the Senate Subcommittee on Multinational Corporations. But observers thought it fairly obvious that the biggest depositors by far were Saudi Arabia and Kuwait. The FRB argued that it had "certain indications to the effect that some of the Arab countries might make large withdrawals if the information on their deposits were publicized." A Treasury official confided that his department disguises the size of Arab holdings of U.S. government securities because "sensitive" Arab regimes had said that disclosure might lead to sudden withdrawals. Powerful bankers journeyed to Washington to warn that the Arabs would pull billions out if their secrecy were penetrated. Felix Rohatyn's prophecy was coming true; the people of the world's greatest capitalist nation did not know who was playing its money markets.

Sudden withdrawals, it turned out, would not be difficult.

About half the Arab funds on deposit had maturities of less than one month.

If one Arab government withdrew its funds from American banks, Chairman Arthur Burns of the Federal Reserve Board told the subcommittee, a fiscal crisis would probably not develop. But if Arab countries acted jointly, "any number of scenarios of hypothetical disaster" could result. Burns did not say so, but all sorts of games are possible. This time the warnings were purely theoretical, but a serious threat—no more, just a threat—of withdrawal of large amounts of cash or assets could put a strain on money markets in the U.S. and/or in Western Europe. As any financial-page reader knows, nothing is quite so prone to panic as the money market.

And there is no reason to doubt that the Arab states, which have already used oil as a weapon and as an avenue to power, would hesitate to use the money weapon against Israel and the West. A former Syrian premier, Salah a-Din al Bitar, gloated quietly over the power of the new weapon; if billions of Arab dollars were to be withdrawn from European banks, he said, this "would give rise to an unprecedented financial crisis in most Western countries." And Fuad Itayim, editor and publisher of the *Middle East Economic Review,* a publication of sobriety, explained the point of it all: "The clients of Arab money may find that they will have to subordinate certain aspects of their foreign policy to their economic self-interest."

While the oil Arabs shifted their great sums from bank to bank, invested billions, spent billions, a historic moment passed almost unnoticed in the late winter of 1975-1976. For the first time in history, imports of oil exceeded production of American wells during a given week. At about the same time, American officialdom let it be known that

Project Independence was not doing sensationally well and it would be foolhardy to think of self-sufficiency in energy for another ten to fifteen years. No one except the Israelis seemed to care.

9

Boycott and Blackmail

The Arab Boycott Office proudly describes itself as an agency almost as old as Israel. Its expressed purpose is the destruction of Israel's economic base through boycott of Israeli products and of foreign firms which trade with Israel or provide Israel with raw materials. Its effects have been felt by Israel in varying degrees through most of the country's life, in such instances as the decision of Renault, the French automobile producers, to discontinue the manufacture of cars in Israel. Still, boycott is an accepted method of exerting pressure and the Arabs used to be low-profit clients whose market for imports was stable but modest. The boycott was widely ignored. Israel, after all, was almost as good a market as all the Arab world together. Israel could—and did—live with the inconveniences the boycott sometimes posed.

The oil pricing crisis of 1973 changed all that. The Arabs, like the wiliest players in an all-night Monopoly game, suddenly owned most of the board. Anyone who wanted to pass GO had to pay—and pay. It paid to pay—the Arabs now had billions upon billions of dollars, German marks, Swiss francs and other assorted hard currency with which to buy things. Buying soared unbelievably. According to the statistics of the Organization for Economic Cooperation and Development (OECD), the average monthly American sales to the Middle East (excluding Israel) rose 109.1 per cent in 1974 and jumped another 82 per cent above that inflated level in 1975; for West Germany, the increases were 100 per cent in 1974 and 96 per cent in 1975; for Sweden 93 per cent and 77 per cent. The price of Arab custom was adherence to the boycott, and growing numbers of profit-oriented companies saw that it made sense to pay the price. And the rules were refined. It was not enough now to avoid dealing with Israeli firms and with companies which bought from or sold to Israel. The quarantine spread to firms across the world which were founded by Jews or employed Jews in key positions. Companies bidding on huge construction jobs suddenly found themselves choosing between multi-million dollar contracts and the hiring of engineers tainted by Judaism. Jewish members of the boards of big corporations found themselves looking from the discouraging graphs of declining corporate profits to the shamed and beseeching faces of their colleagues. Brochures and letterheads were reprinted with the names of Jewish partners notably missing.

The American Jewish Committee, an organization whose members have many links with the business community, pointed to "persistent reports that certain companies have been quietly, on their own initiative, reducing the number of Jews on boards of directors, management or domestic staffs or eliminating them as suppliers or sub-contractors, in hopes of currying favor with actual or potential Arab customers or investors."

Arab investors, one Senator said, were attempting to boycott "so-called Zionist investment banks whose Zionism appears to consist in their having prominent Jewish partners." Chairman Arthur Burns of the Federal Reserve Board saw actions of this kind as a dangerous precedent. Adolf Hitler, he observed, began not by killing Jews but by cutting off their means of livelihood.

It was a world-wide sweep of bigotry. Britain, supine, was an easy victim. There the Saudis introduced a pledge: "We solemnly swear that this company is not a Jewish company, not controlled by Jews or Zionists. . . ." In London, a respected Jewish financier, Sir Max Rayne, was pressured into selling his stock in the merchant bank of Edward Bates after Saudi interests bought up the majority of the shares. An oil company, learning too late that there was a Jewish husband in the private life of a gifted woman employee, withdrew its offer of a promotion to a highly visible post; this led to undesirable newspaper publicity and the company compensated the woman, but the promotion went to someone else. A founding partner of a select British architectural firm retired early, leaving the company—and his non-Jewish partner—free to take on lucrative Arab business. Arab pressure compelled a British bank to exclude the famous houses of S.G. Warburg and B.M. Rothschild from participating in a major loan floated by a Japanese firm. And *The New York Times* printed a telling story about that incident:

> LONDON—A British banker predicted today that the exclusion of Jewish interests from financings involving Arab investors would continue as long as the Arabs wished.
> Gerald Thompson, chairman of Kleinwort, Benson Ltd., one of the leading non-Jewish houses, made it clear that his organization would not resist Arab pressures.

139

His position has implications for the traditional harmony in international banking and for the role of Jewish banks in view of the dollar surpluses accumulating in Arab oil-producing countries.

Some bankers feel that the Arabs' economic power will grow to such an extent that they will eventually dominate the financial markets. The discrimination against Jewish banking interests is cited as an example. A New York merchant bank was also reported on the Arab blacklist.

Reached by telephone at his London office, Mr. Thompson suggested that the banking community was powerless to interfere with the Arab efforts. He ruled out a united front among banks in opposition to the pressures.

Much of the liaison involved in this kind of manipulation of corporate freedom is handled by the central boycott office in Damascus. Its official title is grand and ominous: "League of Arab Countries, General Secretariat, Head Office for the Boycott of Israel, Damascus." It has power to go with that title; it carries the support of the Arab League, a well-healed and tough organization with twenty member states. In mid-1976 King Khalid of Saudi Arabia was blunt and to the point in explaining why his oil fiefdom was a "participant" in the boycott: "For one reason, Saudi Arabia is a member of the Arab League. For another reason, this boycott has proved to be a very effective means of weakening the economy of Israel."

The Boycott Office is headed by a Commissioner General, a very active and eager gentleman named Mohammed Mahmoud Mahgoub. There are regional offices in each Arab state. And delegates from each attend the semi-annual meetings at which the boycott blacklist is reviewed and updated, new business is considered and the plaintive pleas of blacklisted companies to be cleaned are weighed. It is from the regional offices that companies wishing to open business relations in the Arab world receive the affidavit forms which they must fill in to confirm their adherence to the boycott. A sample:

> We hereby certify, under our own responsibility, that our firm, namely   , has no commercial, industrial, and/or any other relations with Israel.
> Our firm does not constitute a branch, subsidiary or main office of any Israeli firm.
> We further declare that we have no direct or indirect interests in all or any Israel concerns, whether government or non-government.

For exporters, there is a certificate of origin, a statement attesting to the fact that no Israeli product has been employed in the manufacture of the item traded. The Boycott Office, a stickler for bureaucratic detail, also expects the freight forwarder and the shipper or airline to make certain—against the risk of being added to the blacklist—that the document accompanies any goods addressed to Arab receivers.

The boycott is a many-faceted affair. It denies Israel the privilege of selling to the Arabs who are their next-door neighbors and natural customers; it forces Israel to search the world for raw materials readily available near at hand in the Arab world; it deprives Israel of the opportunity to earn hard currency by sales in Europe and America; it inhibits know-how agreements, partnerships and many other types of business arrangements. The Boycott Office is well aware that it is fighting a war designed to sap the enemy's strength; Mahgoub has said, with as much honesty as pride, that the boycott is one of the "most strategic weapons" in the Arab arsenal. And, like an army carrying out a major military action, the Boycott Office has the most detailed programming. Its "General Principles for the Boycott of Israel," issued in 1972, consists of thousands of words and scores of meticulous regulations. Here are some of the many rules:

> Aircraft that in the course of their flight to the countries of the Middle East land at an Israeli airport are to be barred from flying over the territory of the Arab states and from being provided with any facilities. . . .

> Foreign persons carrying Israeli visas shall not be permitted to enter the Arab countries. . . .

> Postal parcels arriving in Arab countries and containing gifts for personal use or specimens or commercial samples are exempt from the requirement to submit a certificate of origin provided that . . . all parcels be examined before being released in order to ascertain that their contents do not include Israeli products and that there has entered into them no constituent of Israeli material or workmanship. . . .

> Each Arab state shall intensify the surveillance of banks, financial houses and postal money orders in order to prevent the infiltration of funds from or to Israel. . . .

> It is recommended to the governments of the League of Arab States that they prohibit any Jew who has been deprived of the citizenship of any Arab state that is a member of the League, or whose residence on the soil of such state has been terminated because he has been proved to have had contact or dealings with Occupied Palestine, to enter or reside in the territory of any other Arab state belonging to the League. . . .

> Banned from [customs] free zones are goods and commodities that are Israeli, are consigned to or arriving from Israel, or that contravene the principles of the boycott. . . .

142

. . .The ban is also to be applied with respect to a case of assembly, if it has been established that any Israeli company has assembled a unit of any commodity or goods that goes into components or constituents, the major part of which is produced by a given foreign company or one of its subsidiaries in commercial quantities. . . .

If through convincing material evidence it is confirmed to the boycott organizations that any foreign natural person is a Zionist sympathizer, the following measures are to be taken with respect to him:

1. He shall be inscribed in the list of persons who are forbidden to enter the Arab countries. This is to be done by giving his full name in Latin letters and his nationality.

2. His economic activity is to be watched, and if it is established that he, either alone or with other persons who are known Zionist sympathizers, is the sole owner of a commercial institution or company, and that he or that Zionist person or persons owns 50 percent or more of its capital, the company shall be considered to be pro-Zionist by virtue of the sympathies of its owners. Dealing with it is to be banned as long as these sympathies persist, as is dealing with companies that are considered to be a parent or a subsidiary thereof or controlled by the parent or subsidiary. . . .

4. For the purposes of the application of this recommendation, persons are to be considered as Zionist sympathizers in the following circumstances:
a. If it is established that they are members of associations that have a well-known tendency to act in the interest of world Zionism in general and of the Israeli gangster state in particular. . . .

The Boycott Office does not wish to be considered extreme. Thus, for the sake of "fairness," it has ruled that "the following articles are exempted from the requirement to mention the name of the factory or producing company in certificates of origin, in view of the unfeasibility of arriving at the name of the party producing them:

A. Broken glass.
B. Used non-military woolen clothing.
C. Scrap metal.
D. Scrap rubber.
E. Used tents.
F. Used fiber and burlap bags."

Even taking into account that generous exemption about broken glass, the paperwork which the boycott regulations create can be a Levantine nightmare, as Belvedere Products of Belvedere, Illinois, discovered in 1975 when it tried to get off the blacklist. Mahgoub confirmed that "dealings with [Belvedere] were banned since 1966 because it is a subsidiary of the American company Revlon, Inc., which is banned in all countries of the Arab world," but agreed to consider Belvedere's new status as an independent company, "giving it the chance to resume its business relations with the vast markets of the Arab countries." In addition to the usual disclaimers of association with Israel, however, Mahgoub required: photostats of the company's articles of association; the "names and nationalities" of its shareholders; proof from its bankers that money had actually changed hands in the divorce from Revlon; the "names and nationalities" of Belvedere's board members; the "names and nationalities" of all companies in which Belvedere owned shares both before and after its employees bought the company from Revlon. All these documents would have to be notarized and each and every original would have to be accompanied by twenty-five copies *in Arabic*.

Belvedere's president wrote to his senator, moaning, "I think this is real ridiculous."

According to the General Union of Chambers of Commerce, Industry and Agriculture for Arab Countries, however, the embargo is good for business. A tasteless form letter from the Beirut-based organization explains to Western businessmen that "the Arabs are important customers, for they are rich in purchasing power derived from oil revenues and other sources, whereas their productive capacity is relatively small." Since they cannot import from Israel, they must import from someone else. "Remember, therefore, that Israel is the only loser. . . . However, if no loss is caused to any country, loss may be caused to individual firms. This can happen only when such firms cause themselves to be blacklisted by breaching the regulations of the Arab boycott; but such loss is easily avoidable. The rules themselves are reasonable and, besides, the Arab markets are immensely bigger. . . ."

Companies acceptable to the Arabs exert great care to maintain that happy status. Allied Van Lines International, of Chicago, a major mover of household effects, has put out a brochure for clients which it calls Customs Information. In that section dealing with Arabian [*sic*] countries— specifically identified as Egypt, Jordan, Syria, Iraq, Lebanon, Kuwait, Saudi Arabia and the United Arab Emirates —Allied Van Lines, as quoted at a Senate subcommittee hearing, advised:

> Shippers must check with consulates for approval of items to be brought into the country. Items produced in Israel or by Jewish firms or associates throughout the world are blacklisted.

The Senate Banking Committee, in an official report on the boycott, commented: "The implication that Allied would not ship the products of *Jewish,* not necessarily Israeli, firms to Arab states was clear."

The Senate committee also provided graphic evidence of

the Boycott Office's ability to strike fear among the executives, symbols of free enterprise, of major American companies. It told the story of a manufacturer—unnamed but obviously of respectable size—with a contract to supply buses to an Arab state: ". . . after the bus manufacturer placed an order with one of its suppliers to supply seats for the buses, it was advised that the supplier was on the Arab blacklist and that, as a consequence, buses incorporating seats made by the supplier would not be acceptable. The manufacturer's order with its supplier was subsequently terminated." U.S. firms, the Banking Committee concluded angrily, "are thus put in the position of discriminating against other U.S. firms pursuant to the dictates of foreign governments."

Business documents provided to a Senate investigating subcommittee included a set of "invoice instructions" from Getty Oil's Houston office, saying: "We certify that the goods listed are not of Israeli origin nor do they contain any Israeli materials." A standard letter from the Peralta shipping firm of New York was placed in the record: "We, the undersigned, certify that the vessel on the bill of lading is not the property of Israel or an Israeli subject and is not a blacklisted ship. In addition, this vessel, even if not belonging to Israel or to an Israeli subject, is not scheduled to call at an Israeli port before the discharge of the merchandise at the port of _____." Similar letters were produced on the stationery of other shipping firms: Waterman, Lykes Bros., Boise-Griffin, Cross-Ocean, Kerr, Hellenic, Barberlines, State Marine-Isthmian. American Export-Isbrandtsen cautiously sought to protect itself against acts of God: "This vessel is not to call at any Israeli port and will not pass through the territorial waters of Israeli [sic], prior to unloading in Lebanon unless the ship is in distress or subject to *Force Majeure*."

146

There was also a letter from the Bankers Trust Co., one of New York's biggest, informing an exporter that it had authority to pay $2,419 for chemicals shipped to the University of Tripoli, Libya, against presentation of papers including a declaration that the chemical-producing company was in no way linked with Israel. Later, the Anti-Defamation League of B'nai B'rith, an organization which fights discrimination wherever it surfaces, charged that Bankers Trust and twenty-four other large commercial banks, including such giants as Chase Manhattan, Morgan Guaranty Trust, Bank of America and Citibank, were participating in the boycott by processing "boycott-tainted letters of credit."

But criticisms of the boycott were just a bore to much of the business community. In August, 1976, high-ranking officials of three hundred industrial corporations gathered on the campus of the University of Maine for a week-long Mideast-American Business Conference. The attendance fee alone was $1,000 per man. Obviously, this was chicken feed. For, as the president of the U.S.-Arab Chamber of Commerce pointed out, "The Middle East is where the action is." He buttressed that statement with a statistic and an estimate—that U.S. goods shipped to the Arab world rose in value from $1 billion in 1972 to $5.5 billion in 1975, and would soon hit $10 billion. A gentleman from Qatar, one of 150 representatives of twelve Arab states gracing the conference, said: "We need anything you can think of, from toothpaste to heavy equipment." After that, it was no burden to attend a special session where Arab League officials discussed the boycott, its legal framework and how to get off the blacklist. In that last connection, *The Washington Post* quoted a realistic federal bureaucrat: "There is only one way we know to get delisted, and that is to stop doing business with Israel."

147

It was, by some indications, quite the thing to do. A self-satisfied Mohammed Mahgoub wrote in 1975: "I would like to stress the fact that companies which settle their status and have their names deleted from the blacklist are seven or eight times as many as those whose names are on the list."

The boycott has had the cooperation of the U.S. Army and the U.S. Departments of State, Commerce and Treasury. Many American commercial firms, like companies the world over, have chosen to comply with the boycott for profit. Government agencies were doing the Arabs a favor and, they claimed, fulfilling compulsions of state. The U.S. Army Corps of Engineers has been acting as management consultant, planner and contractor for Saudi Arabia for two decades, designing and building installations—airfields, television systems, military cantonments, port facilities—costing many millions of dollars. At the insistence of the Saudis, the Corps always screened out Jews when filling jobs in Saudi Arabia. Two corps officers admitted that under Congressional questioning in 1975. One of them said: "The Arabs make the rules, and it would be unwise to send a Jew out there."

The State Department deals with this purblind Arab bigotry by obligingly eliminating Jews from consideration when foreign service posts fall vacant in Arab countries. In the early 1970s, the State Department sought to hide this discriminatory practice by officially expunging from the records all references to the religious affiliations of its employees. It is a legal fiction which has no practical effect; everyone at the State Department knows who's who. Still, department spokesmen have turned aside questions about discrimination in Middle Eastern postings by insisting that the State Department does not even know who's Jewish any more. At one briefing in late 1975, however, the departmental spokesman was forced to the mat by determined journalistic questioners who demanded to know how many Jewish foreign service officers were actually serving in, say, Saudi Arabia. The spokesman fidgeted and then said he did not think there were any.

Deputy Assistant Secretary of State Harold Saunders was more imaginative about the question of Jewish visitors to the vastness of Saudi Arabia when he appeared before the Church committee:

> *Mr. Saunders:* We have people who do go in and out of Saudi Arabia in connection with U.S. Government business who are Jewish. Yes, sir.
> *Sen. Church:* State Department personnel?
> *Mr. Saunders:* Yes, sir.
> *Sen. Church:* Secretary Kissinger?
> *Mr. Saunders:* I am not being facetious by having him only in mind. That is true.

Rep. Henry Waxman (D-Calif.) did not have Kissinger's influence. Waxman, planning to join a House subcommittee on a Middle East mission, sent a staff aide to the Saudi Embassy in Washington to apply for a visa. All went well until the aide, having been asked for a letter from a minister attesting to Waxman's religious affiliation, naïvely appeared with a letter from a rabbi. That did it; the visa was refused on the spot. And Waxman got into Saudi Arabia only through the personal intervention of the American Ambassador. When the group had an audience with the Saudi king, the persistent Waxman asked about Saudi policy toward Jews. The king angrily replied: "The Jews have no business in Saudi Arabia. They are our enemies. Jews from America and around the world support Israel. Friends of our enemies are our enemies."

Only a few months earlier the U.S. and Saudi governments had signed a set of economic and military cooperation agreements at a ceremony in Washington. The ever-present Dr. Kissinger called the agreements "a milestone in our relations."

Certainly, the economic accord was wide-ranging. It established a joint governmental commission, plus an economic council to foster cooperation in the field of finance. The whole apparatus was to serve as the vehicle for channeling billions of dollars of new business into Saudi Arabia. Everything was fine, except for one small point. The document signed by Henry Kissinger and the Saudi King's half-brother pledged that the joint programs would be "sensitive to the social, cultural, political and religious contexts of Saudi Arabia."

That sounded like a code-phrase for prejudice, and the Administration moved with ponderous slowness to cool the resultant liberal anger. Many months passed before Secretary of Treasury William Simon, returning from a mission to Riyadh, quietly spread the word (a public announcement might have upset the Saudis) that there would be no discrimination on the grounds of sex, color, religion, etc., against any American working under the aegis of the joint economic commission. That left much unsettled. There was no way of knowing whether the Treasury or subcontractors would follow the precedent set by the Corps and the State Department and weed out Jews from among those destined to work in the Saudi wilderness. The agreement did not cover Americans lacking the commission's blessing. And, obviously, it did not assure that companies tainted with Jewish or Zionist influence would have equal access to Saudi or commission business.

The executive branch of the U.S. Government considers opposition to the boycott bad for business. An Undersecretary of Commerce, arguing against proposed anti-boycott legislation, said that, if the Arab countries "found themselves unable to obtain the assurances they seek in trading with American companies, they would just take their business elsewhere and purchase from other countries." (The truth was that the Arabs, when they needed something badly enough, always ignored the boycott.) An Assistant Secretary of Treasury, Gerald L. Parsky, took the broad, statesmanlike approach: "The boycott arose out of the Arab-Israel conflict and continues to be viewed as part of that conflict. We believe it can best be resolved through a peaceful settlement in the Middle East and not by imposing or threatening to impose restrictions on economic ties."

In spirit, that statement is a violation of the Export Administration Act adopted by Congress in 1969. The act proclaimed: "It is the policy of the United States to oppose restrictive trade practices or boycotts fostered or imposed by foreign countries against other countries friendly to the United States." The only trouble was, the act had no teeth. It is simply a statement of principle, of intent, not a ban on compliance with the boycott. The Commerce and Treasury Departments opposed all thought of giving the act enforcement powers or penalty provisions. For years, the official Commerce Department notice to businessmen about boycott policy flashed a clear signal: ". . .You are not legally prohibited from taking action, including the furnishing of information or the signing of agreements that have the effect of furthering or supporting such restrictive practices or boycotts."

There is no impressive body of evidence to illustrate that the federal executive branch fights the noble fight to get blacklisted companies off the Arab boycott list. In mid-1974 top executives of CBS, Coca-Cola, Ford, Monsanto, Motorola, RCA, Republic Steel and Whirlpool—all on the Arab blacklist—sent Kissinger a note of congratulations on his Middle East diplomacy and then got to the point: "As efforts go forward to develop normal relations in the Middle East, it appears to us that there is no longer a place for the Arab boycott against U.S. companies which, as part of their normal international activity, have been engaged in business with customers in Israel." Nothing happened. The State Department continued to cling to the proposition that the way to end the boycott was to end the war, an interesting proposition since the war had gone on for three decades and could last another three.

The Export Administration Act did require exporters to report boycott requests to the Commerce Department. The figures tell a grim story of escalating Arab power and dwindling American courage. In 1974, according to reports filed with the Department by U.S. firms, there were 785 export transactions involving an Arab demand for compliance with the boycott. In the first three quarters of 1975 there were 7,545 such transactions, nearly a ten-fold increase. The number of U.S. companies reporting receipt of boycott demands in January through September, 1975, was twenty-three times the total for 1974. The dollar value of the transactions jumped more than twenty times.

The firms at that time were not required to disclose how they were reacting to the Arab demands, but voluntary statements showed that they were putting profit above principles of free trade in more than half the transactions in the 1975 period. In the third quarter of 1975, there was stated readiness to surrender to the Arabs in more than 63 per cent of the transactions. The true persuasiveness of the boycott became evident when Commerce, yielding to public pressure, grudgingly changed the rules to compel exporters to disclose their responses beginning October 1, 1975. In the next half year there were 24,710 transactions, for a total value of $1.7 billion, involving demands for boycott adherence. U.S. businessmen bowed to the Arabs in 22,481 instances, or 90.9 per cent.

The Commerce Department's set of categories of "restrictive trade practices by Arab states against Israel," drawn up by bloodless bureaucrats interested in reality, not principles, was itself revealing as to the scope of the economic war against Israel:

   a. Certification that exporter has no subsidiaries or financial interest in Israel.
   b. Certification that carrying vessel is not blacklisted.
   c. Certification that insurance company is not blacklisted.
   d. Certification that goods are of pure origin of the exporting state.
   e. Certification that goods are not of Israeli origin and contain no material of Israeli origin.
   f. Certification that West German reparation of Israel is not involved.
   g. Other.

The Senate Banking Committee, having studied the department's statistics, warned that the boycott's "power and reach promise to grow further as trade and investment with the West expand." The statement was a simple truth. Involved in boycott compliance were some of the biggest companies in the United States, supposedly no easy prey to blackmail by countries which badly needed what the giant and sophisticated firms had to peddle. The price paid for an Arab certificate of cleanliness included some singular departures from integrity, as in the case of the giant bank with billions in assets (First National City) which printed a Middle East economic survey accompanied by a map from which Israel's name was omitted—because Israel's existence offends Arab sensibilities and that is bad for business.

With so much money and so much power involved, things were bound to get complicated. For example, there was the case of the Bechtel construction company. Its record was not really in question. Bechtel "invoicing instructions," reproduced in the transcript of a Senate subcommittee hearing, stated:

> Invoices must bear the following certification:
> We hereby certify that the goods enumerated in this invoice are not of Israeli origin nor do they contain any Israeli materials nor were they shipped on vessels boycotted by the Israeli [*i.e.* Arab] Boycott Office nor were they designated to visit an Israeli port nor were they exported from Israel.

Bechtel was the world's largest construction company, vast and powerful, with hundreds of millions of dollars in contracts and extensive business connections in the Arab world. Its president was George P. Schultz, former Secretary of the Treasury. It had helped build the great Tapline and laid thousands of miles of other oil pipelines across the Arab deserts. It had many friends both in the Arab world and in Washington. When the Justice Department decided to make Bechtel a test case of boycott legality, other bureaucrats were both surprised and angered. Henry Kissinger found time while in China to cable the Attorney General and reportedly argued that the suit would "adversely affect" American foreign policy and the peace-making process. The Justice Department, undeterred, filed its suit, basing its case on the Sherman Anti-Trust Act because there was none more relevant, no newer law to cope with Bechtel's dealings with the Arabs. Bechtel did not deny adherence to the boycott and simply claimed that it was acting legally in complying with the laws of the Arab countries with which it did business. The question would take years to work its way through the courts. Meanwhile, Bechtel was *not* enjoined from its adherence to the boycott. Nor was Bechtel, the world's biggest contractor, in the federal doghouse; after the suit was filed, Gerald Ford gave a State dinner for Jordan's King Hussein and the White House guest list included the name of Stanley Bechtel of the Bechtel Group of Companies.

Bechtel may well have considered its treatment by Justice unfair. For years, the Commerce Department had been routinely circulating Arab tenders—invitations for bids—among American businessmen with a covering note: "The following trade opportunities have been submitted to the Department of Commerce by U.S. foreign service posts overseas." Those documents were hardly proclamations of goodwill. Roderick Hills, chairman of the Securities and Exchange Commission, was to testify later: "They had the most venal kind of representations in them, such as, 'Would you sign and certify that your company is not Jewish; that you have no Jews on your board of directors?' That was a most degrading activity, I think, for companies and for our government to be involved in."

One tender which focused on Israel finally fell into the hands of the Anti-Defamation League. It was a detailed communication from the Iraqi government, which wanted to buy 3,550 pre-fabs of pre-cast cement. Paragraph 13 of the Iraqi tender read: "Country of Origin: The tenderers shall not incorporate [in] this tender any material that has been manufactured in Israel or by companies boycotted officially by [the] Iraqi government."

The ADL protested and said that the action by the Commerce Department, which is "charged with enforcing" the Export Administration Act, actually "promotes, supports, aids and abets the anti-Jewish and anti-Israel boycott."

155

There was pious shock in the halls of the Commerce Department. "We were quite disturbed," a Deputy Assistant Secretary wrote the ADL, "to learn that, contrary to long-standing Departmental policy, copies of this tender and other trade opportunity documents were disseminated without attaching thereto a statement of United States policy opposing such restrictive trade practices and requesting the American firms concerned not to comply with them. . . . We do not believe that any useful purpose would be served if the Department of Commerce refused to disseminate bid invitations subject to restrictive clauses, thereby denying U.S. firms prompt access to business opportunities in the Arab markets which they are lawfully permitted to pursue."

"Business opportunities," the Anti-Defamation League pointed out, happened to be a weapon in somebody else's war and the U.S. government was helping to punish the innocent bystanders. The Commerce Department finally acceded and tenders with boycott riders no longer go out with their imprimatur. The Arabs send them out themselves. There's no law against it.

If the Arabs have their way, there will never be such a law. Saudi Arabia blames efforts to deal with boycott discrimination in the courts as Israeli attempts to "break the Saudis." Accompanying this piquant inversion of boycotter and victim are low mutterings of impending oil shortages; threats of loss of business totaling (a possibly highly inflated figure of) $30 billion; sorrowful regrets at the patent impossibility of investing in an ingrate country like the U.S. and the usual cracks about the Zionist lobby. A story embodying all this and more came out of Riyadh in the winter of 1976 and the *Washington Post* printed it with the headline: ANTI-ARAB BOYCOTT MOVES IN U.S. IMPERIL CONTRACTS WITH SAUDIS.

These were the moves which so aroused the wrath of Saudi Arabia that it threatened the very continuation of trade with its old and valued ally: The government was looking at the boycott and the Sherman Anti-Trust Act to see whether U.S. corporations were being illegally squeezed. The chairman of the Federal Reserve Board had sent notices to 5,800 member-banks cautioning them against acting as agents of the boycott. The suit against Bechtel had been filed. The American Jewish Congress, in a class action, was suing the Treasury, the State Department, the Commerce Department and the Joint Commission on Economic Cooperation, claiming that all assisted in discriminating against American Jews who cannot obtain visas to Saudi Arabia.

The Saudi Minister of Industry, Ghazi Abdul Rahman Qusaibi, viewed these actions with sorrow: "We have our boycott legislation and do not intend to change it."

If there was applause for this statement of faith, it did not come from any of the 1,500 American companies, individuals and organizations on the Saudi blacklist alone. Inclusion on this or similar but not necessarily identical blacklists maintained by other Arab countries is sometimes whimsical; all that's needed, in Mahgoub's words, is proof that the companies, "their proprietors or controllers have Zionist inclinations." The Saudi list included, in no particular order, Fairbanks Morse, Pratt & Whitney, Harry Belafonte, Xerox, Hartz Mountain Pet Food, Burlington Industries, Connecticut Mutual, International Latex, Henri Bendel, Lazard Frères, Kaiser Aluminum, Frank Sinatra, All-State Insurance, Kennebec Paper, Zenith Radio, Sears Roebuck, Baker's Infant Formula, Engelhard Minerals and Chemicals, Paul Masson, Reynolds Construction, Omar Sharif and such naturals as the American Jewish Congress, the American Jewish Committee, the Anti-Defamation League and the Commission on Education of the United Synagogues of America.

There couldn't be any applause, either, from the State of California. That entity had already gotten its dose of what Qusaibi was talking about. During the worst of a recent recession, the Saudis had come forward with an attractive deal just as the decision was being taken to lay off 10 per cent of the highway workers on the State payroll. The Saudis had $25 million floating around and plans for a massive highway construction program. They would even take the California workers under an arrangement which would permit their technical continuation on the California work rolls; seniority and retirement rights would be protected.

Then came word that the Saudis did not want Blacks, or women staffers, or Jews. There was consternation in the State House, and the Saudi Embassy in Washington immediately backtracked. They would take Blacks and women, they said. It was Zionists they did not want.

California's labor code specifically restrains the state from entering into any contacts involving discrimination based on race, sex, religion or national origin. The governor's legal secretary was therefore dispatched to Washington to consult the State Department and ask the Saudis the $25,000,000 question: What is a Zionist? It took a week and "a lot of euphemisms and abstract concepts," the emissary was to say later, "but in the end, I think that, realistically, the Saudi government defines Zionists as all Jews." With that, the contract talks ended. Saudi Arabia had its boycott legislation and did not intend to change it.

It was not an incident designed to make friends for Arabs in California, but the Arabs are no longer in a position where they care whether they are loved or not. Money is power. The boycott, as a weapon in the war against Israel, is beginning to pay off and the good folk of the Arab world can be expected to turn the screws harder with each victory in their stubborn struggle to accomplish the economic destruction of Israel.

They have their useful allies. When Chairman Burns of the Federal Reserve Board warned U.S. banks against boycott-tainted letters of credit, the banks and three Federal departments—State, Commerce and Treasury—were shocked but not paralyzed. They mounted extreme pressure, and the FRB had to yield. It was handled with bureaucratic finesse. The warning was not rescinded, but a clarification was issued saying the "initial letter was not intended to create a new legal obligation for banks," and adding that prime responsibility for U.S. policy on the boycott lay with the Commerce Department. Since Commerce's record was thoroughly clear, the banks felt much better. The American Jewish Congress felt much worse; it issued a statement that said the banks were continuing the practice of issuing discriminatory and restrictive letters of credit and it blasted the banking industry's "craven surrender to the Arab boycott." If the banks noticed, they paid no attention. Indeed, a Federal survey of 119 banks for the December 1975–March 1976 period showed that the banks had complied with boycott requests at a rate averaging more than one thousand a month and altogether had turned down a grand total of 288 such requests. One big bank acknowledged that it had participated in 824 letters of credit involving $41.2 million in boycott-tainted business in that period.

A baffled Rep. Robert Drinan, a Massachusetts Democrat and a Jesuit, questioned a Chemical Bank vice-president, Edwin E. Batch, Jr., about all this at a congressional hearing.

MR DRINAN: This is simply obvious and open discrimination against Israel . . . In banking circles, do people dis-

159

cuss this and say, "Why can't we all rise above this and just set it aside?" . . . .

MR. BATCH: We have discussed the legal aspects of the regulations and the law.

MR. DRINAN: But never the moral aspects. You don't care about morality?

MR. BATCH: No; we are not talking about moral issues here. You are really asking if the banks get together and discuss what they will do about this boycott clause. That is an antitrust situation.

MR. DRINAN: But you just stay with the legal aspect. If it is legal, then it is okay. You don't care about morality.

MR. BATCH: That is precisely my job.

"It is clear to me," Burns wrote a congressional subcommittee half a year after his reform effort was torpedoed, "that banks in the United States play a crucial role in giving effect to the Arab boycott in this country." The Federal Reserve Chairman urged Congress toward remedial action.

And Congress did try its best, making a major effort in mid-1976 to strengthen the Export Administration Act, then about to expire. The Senate passed a bill to forbid firms from refusing to do business with a company simply because the latter was on the Arab blacklist, and the House drafted even tougher legislation. But the Ford Administration, in its anxiety not to offend the oil Arabs or U.S. business supporters, fought back with fury; the Arabs threatened economic retaliation; Mobil Oil bought a full-page ad in the *New York Times* to raise the spectre of a new oil crisis; lobbyists for Standard Oil of California, Bechtel, Caterpillar Tractor, the National Association of Manufacturers and other interested parties were pointedly on hand in the Capitol hallway when representatives of the two chambers met to reconcile the two bills; a Texas oil Senator threw up parliamentary obstacles. Not surprisingly, the amended legislation was still-born when Congress adjourned for the 1976 campaign. The Export Administration Act, inadequate as it was, expired and was replaced by a still weaker Executive Order. Gerald Ford, hard-pressed in a TV debate with his Democratic opponent, grandly announced a decision to make public specific boycott demands and company responses to them, but the subsequent Commerce regulations applied only to the future, not the telling past record, and permitted continued confidentiality on the meaningful facts—the amount of money involved, the type of goods, the quantity of goods. There was, in other words, sound but no substance.

The months of congressional anti-boycott work had only one slender result: a tax law provision lifting certain tax benefits from that portion of a firm's business involving boycott-tainted sales. A businessman's conference on the boycott (and coping with it), held even before the tax provision became law, heard the practical suggestion that companies explore the idea of transacting business with the Arabs through subsidiaries abroad or middlemen. It was safer that way. A summation of the meeting, as disclosed by a congressional subcommittee, quoted an ingenious Commerce representative to this effect: ". . . if a U.S. company's foreign affiliate receives a boycott request and does not report it to the U.S. parent, the U.S. parent is not expected to report the request to the Commerce Department."

Some other recent Arab victories: In 1974, U.S.-Canadian private investment in Israel dropped by more than half, and the recession was not the only reason. One financial expert in New York spoke contemptuously of giant companies hastening to assure potential Arab customers of their new-found anti-Israel bias before the Arabs even thought to ask. In Britain, shipbuilders turned unaccountably gelid

161

when a plump $7 million Israeli contract for tugboats was offered for bids. Governments themselves turned timid; when Arab financiers prevailed upon a *nationalized* French bank to drop the prestigious Jewish firm of Lazard Frères from a syndicate arranging a loan for *government*-owned Air France, the French Premier, his eyes, doubtless, innocently wide, saw no way to "adopt a constraining attitude one way or the other." Some perennial exhibitors at Tel Aviv's annual industrial fair stopped coming. Only one of the car manufacturers of Japan, a country heavily dependent on Arab oil and eager for the recycling of those Arab petrodollars, was willing to sell its products in Israel. The Belgian purchasing office of an American chemical firm turned down as "too high" a tender from a long-time Israeli supplier whose prices and service until then had always been above reproach, and turned the Israeli firm down again when the price was lowered a full 20 per cent. The European subsidiary of a Canadian company suddenly refused to deliver an Israeli order of heavy metals, declining to explain why. Electronic communications equipment was available in Britain to everyone but the Israeli postal service—at a time when the British were looking everywhere for export markets.

All this is on the record. It is the work of fearful people faced by blackmail by the oil-producing Arab states who now hold control of an estimated *one-fifth* of the world's surplus resources, an utterly staggering heap of money. The Arabs have now placed the full weight of their riches on one side of the scale. This spells incalculable danger to Israel, but it also carries with it a measure of disaster for the West. Corporations orchestrated by the likes of the Commissioner General of the Arab Central Boycott Office may be enterprising, but they are no longer free. There is more to be lost to the Arabs in this instance than the viability of Israel.

In judging the impact on Israel itself, however, it is necessary to think not in political or moral terms but in the harsh terms of economic reality and of the practices and thought processes of the business world. It is not a question principally of what companies *do* but of what they *fail* to do. Lest that sound puzzling, consider the facts: Israel is a small country hampered by three decades of war and the need for constant preparedness, spending a larger percentage of its Gross National Product on defense *than any other country in the world.* Because of the Arab boycott it cannot play its natural economic role, dictated by geography, as a center for Middle Eastern trade and processor of Middle Eastern raw materials. Its principal natural resource is the skills of its people. Like all nations but more than most, it must make its economy grow—or die. Given its unique situation as a pariah in its habitat, Israel can grow only by developing a sophisticated economy geared to the markets beyond the Arab Crescent. That means developing industries which are capital-intensive, skilled labor-intensive, science-intensive. To do that in a world grown increasingly competitive and complex, Israel needs the help of Western capital, Western know-how, Western licensing agreements and Western partnerships. It is exactly here that the Arab boycott hurts the most. Western firms, faced with the knowledge that cooperation with Israel will be at the risk of the loss of Arab custom, simply avoid making deals with Israel. Why choose trouble, especially when there is more profit among all those petrodollars anyway?

Firm examples of this negative approach to Israel are sometimes difficult to pinpoint because the problem does not involve decisions but the avoidance of decisions. Some

163

evidence, however, is available. Israel had reason to believe that, a deal made, after years of negotiations, with the Common Market to eliminate all tariffs on Israeli-manufactured goods would stimulate American firms into opening subsidiaries in Israel, using Israel's skilled and relatively inexpensive labor to produce for the European market; but the stampede of American businessmen failed to develop. An American company big enough to be on the Fortune 100 list has relationships with Israel, and economic logic dictates that those relations grow; instead, they are dwindling and the company seems to be slowly phasing out of Israel. Engineering firms carefully detour around Israel. Architectural consulting firms, dazzled by the prospect of building castles in the Saudi sands, would just as soon not enter the Israeli market. It is no accident that only one major American chemical company—Monsanto—is seriously active in Israel.

The General Tire & Rubber Co. of Akron provides an illustrative case history. General Tire was on the Arab blacklist because it had once held a one-third equity in a tire company in Israel. It sold its shares in 1963 but, despite strenuous efforts, did not get off the blacklist until 1973. Later, it was disclosed that to get off the list, General Tire had paid $150,000 to a Lebanese-based conglomerate run by Adnan Khashoggi, a fast-moving, fast-talking, self-made Saudi multi-millionaire with the right contacts in the right places.

Exchanges of money for services rendered are not so unusual in the world of business; a General Tire executive said the $150,000 exchange was a legitimate business transaction. What was germane about the General Tire case was a charge made by the Securities and Exchange Commission as a result of its investigation of a spate of foreign payoffs. General Tire, the SEC charged, had failed to disclose that in 1971 it had filed a sworn certificate with the Arab League stating that the company and its subsidiaries would not provide any technical service or know-how to any Israeli company and that its subsidiary, Aerojet General, would neither invest in Israel nor furnish any technical assistance to Israeli industry. As often happens in such cases, General Tire neither admitted nor denied the series of SEC charges but agreed to a court injunction barring future violations of law.

The boycott, with its overtones both of racism and of unreasoning, uncompromising, unending war with Israel, can be embarrassing to a country such as Egypt, trying so hard to project an image of peacefulness and reason in order to win American loans, arms, grants, investments and diplomatic support. In 1976, Ashraf Ghorbal, Egypt's suave Ambassador to Washington, tried to explain the boycott's motivations to a business-oriented American periodical: "Israeli occupation of Arab lands and violation of legitimate Palestinian rights constitute an act of belligerency which forces the Arab states to resort to the Arab boycott." If Ghorbal's readers tried to analyze those words, they would probably have concluded that he was saying the boycott was a result of the 1967 war when, to avoid attack, Israel staged a pre-emptive attack, and so had nothing to do with the fundamental Arab rejection of Israel. The readers could hardly be expected to know what Ghorbal knew— that the boycott was first launched in 1945 against the fledgling Jewish community of Palestine, renewed in 1947 to thwart a UN decision to partition Palestine into two states, renewed again against a new-born nation with which Egypt and three other Arab states had actually signed a binding armistice, and maintained for decades as part of the overall offensive against Israel's life.

Ghorbal's words were distributed across America courtesy of *U.S. News & World Report.* Almost no one in the United States read the editorial in a newspaper in the Jordanian capital of Amman a couple of months earlier which complained about anti-boycott moves in the U.S. and Britain and commented: "The Israeli sharks scenting fresh blood are circling around their victim for the kill." (The metaphor was not easy to follow, but the apparent victim was the government and/or business community of the United States and/or Britain.) The editorial said the boycott "did not start in 1967" but "was envisaged the day Israel was created." The editorialist was proud to be able to add: "Furthermore, Arab countries not directly involved in the 1967 war with Israel are party to the boycott drive. . . ."

The point of it all was: Do not relax the boycott. Instead, intensify it. The war continues. "The instrument of war this time," as Israel's Foreign Minister Yigal Allon aptly put it in a parliamentary statement, "isn't the tank and the concentration camp but the check and the petrodollar."

10

*F*riends at *H*ome

The Arab Information Centers, housed in well-appointed offices in New York, San Francisco, Chicago, Dallas and Washington, D.C., are busily engaged in spreading the lies the Arabs use to subvert public opinion in the United States. They claim to be working "to counter Zionist influence." Actually, the goal of the Arab information network goes far beyond that. The sole purpose of these Centers is to undermine and destroy Israel.

A mile or so from the White House, the Washington Arab Information Center displays neatly stacked leaflets whose covers are adorned with the dove of peace or pictures of smiling children. Inside, the message reads "war." One booklet contains the flat statement that "most Palestinians" would consider an Arab state on the West Bank and the Gaza Strip to be "a minimum medium-run political goal," a jargon phrase for an interim state which would proceed to eliminate Israel. A collection of essays published by the Arab Information Center, titled "Toward

167

Peace in Palestine,'' includes a piece by Said Hammami, a
PLO functionary based in London, which expresses the
hope that "one day this interloper state will disappear from
the scene in the Middle East.'' Hammami points to the diffi-
culties of a "non-violent and evolutionary" process to
accomplish this end, explaining that even after the establishment of a mini-state "it might not be possible to rule out
entirely continued sporadic acts of violence by individuals
driven to desperation by continued injustice on the part of
Israel under Zionist leadership.'' Such code language is
also used in an essay by Hatim Hussaini, an official of the
Arab League, who opines that solutions like "dividing the
country into two are not based on real coexistence and true
equality and thus would no doubt lead to future conflict and
war. . . . The liberation of Palestine must be total.''

Through their Information Centers, the Arabs routinely
arrange for speakers to talk before church and civic groups
and in TV studios on such subjects as the Arab refugees,
promoting the old line. The campaign is directed at the
broad spectrum of the influential public, focusing on black
Americans, teachers, professionals, trade unionists and
academics in particular. Few listeners ever know that the
pious speaker on the podium is being paid by a front for the
League of Arab States, the organization which inaugurated
and operates the boycott of Israel. Nor does the audience
necessarily know that the Arab League spends $1 million a
year on PLO operations in the U.S. alone; that it is the
creation of twenty Arab countries dedicated to the eradication of an American ally and that it has been up to its neck
in violence and bloodshed since its inception.

The political, military and propaganda-coordinating body
of the Arab world, the League is reportedly spending $30
million a year on anti-Israel propaganda in the United
States alone. Some of its money has been paid to at least

two Madison Avenue public relations firms who were commissioned to sugarcoat the Arab message of destruction to make it more palatable to the American public. Their expertise has resulted in a dramatic change of approach.

In 1970, for example, the Arab League brought a Lebanese journalist, Clovis Maksoud, to the United States on a speaking tour. He was a firebrand. Wherever he appeared, he denounced the very notion of an Arab Palestinian state which could co-exist with the State of Israel. It was unthinkable because, Maksoud said, such a move would lend "legitimacy to the Zionist state of Israel in the midst of the Arab nation." It was a harsh message for which Americans were unprepared. Maksoud was not a success.

Four years later, when the Arab League brought him back, he was a changed man with a new and ostensibly softer line. This time he talked about the rights of all peoples in the Middle East to coexist in a democratic society. He was so convincing that he was returned to the American lecture circuit the next year. He now advocated the creation of an Arab state in part of Palestine—a position that represented a turn of 180 degrees from the one he advocated in his fiery speeches of the past. Once such an Arab state was founded, Maksoud told college students, newspaper editors and congressmen, there would arise "an historic opportunity to move into an ultimate reconciliation" between Jews and Arabs. And this would happen "as a consequence of persuasion and not of confrontation. This is the meaning of the democratic state of Palestine."

But the new public-relations line glossed over the period of "persuasion" between the establishment of an Arab state side-by-side with Israel and the emergence of a single "democratic state of Palestine." Maksoud covered it in an emotional statement which ignored the centuries of persecution visited upon the Jews in the Arab world: "Our basic

169

objection to Israel is that it tries to tear Judaism away from our heritage and to tear the Jews away from being part of our destiny." Then came the give-away, the new line devised to cloak the genocidal intent of the projected Arab state. It was phrased as a rhetorical question: "Do the Arabs . . . have to accept the inevitability of Jewish alienation? Do they have to accept that the Jews, per se, have a right to exist as a nation permanently?" The rhetorical answer: "We do not concede that religion or even ethnicity are the sole criteria for nationhood."

Maksoud's words, had his audiences known it, were the new code for the relegation of Jews to their old position of subjugation to Islam. And they led straight back to the tenets of the Palestine Liberation Organization, whose entire philosophy rests on the right of the Arabs alone to a national identity in the area that now calls itself Israel.

Clovis Maksoud, in fact, was no stranger to the PLO or even to Yasir Arafat himself. In the spring of 1975, as two jeeps manned with heavy machine guns stood guard outside and "there were men and boys with guns all over the place," Maksoud acted as interpreter in an interview which Arafat granted to the American columnist Joseph Kraft in Beirut.

"As to the long-term," Kraft wrote, "Arafat flatly refused to say that the PLO would ever renounce the use of force against a Jewish state in Palestine. When I rose to leave, he said: 'I hope we meet again in a secular democratic state where Moslems, Jews and Christians can live together in peace.'"

Maksoud himself, not unlike Arafat, got right to the point when talking for home consumption. In between lecture tours in the U.S., he told an Arabic publication in Beirut that "the next stage of the Arab-Israel conflict" should feature a campaign "to deprive Zionism of the support of world Jewry." He considered this a concept with marvelous possibilities: "If we succeed, it means the end of the idea [of] and the state of Israel."

The Arab League spends a fortune in the United States to supply Arab fronts, pro-Arab lobby groups and anyone else who will pay attention with slickly written and taped materials. It finances the research and publication or distribution of hard-cover, pro-PLO tracts. The Madison Avenue expertise of American marketing minds is increasingly to be found in the carefully worded leaflets the League distributes, the open letters it sends to the media and the ads it inserts in the press at opportune moments.

The Arab Information Center in Washington helps spread the benign message with a biweekly newsletter, *Arab Report,* which is mailed to journalists and opinion-makers. It is skillfully printed in two colors on the best paper and is conservative in make-up and design; it strives for dignity in words as well as production. But occasionally *Arab Report*'s editors forget themselves. In the June 1, 1976, issue, at a time when the civil war in Lebanon was taking hundreds of innocent lives a week and just before Arab gunmen in Beirut coldly murdered the American Ambassador, one of his aides and his Arab chauffeur, *Arab Report* wrote of "Israeli killers on the loose in major Palestinian cities murdering people at will." The country in which these killers lived was not a nation but "the Israeli entity." The residents of that "entity" were "sawdust colonialist squatters . . . who have nothing but contempt for the Arab world."

On the other hand, during the Arab oil embargo, while New Englanders were jobless, oil prices were being rigged and motorists lined up for hours at gas stations, an Arab League advertisement spoke in tones of smooth reason to agitated Americans. Its message: there was an ocean of oil

171

to be tapped and profits aplenty, too, for Americans in the Middle East—and all that stood in the way was Israel.

"We want," proclaimed one full-page ad published in major newspapers across the U.S., "to sell our oil, our greatest single source of revenue. Income from oil is financing our vital development projects. Our imports will increase as the pace of development quickens. Thus, except for America's unquestioning support for Israel, there is a mutuality of interests between us and the U.S."

In that same period, an organization called Americans for Middle East Understanding was sending out a massive mailing to the members of the pivotal interstate trucking industry. The truckers were feeling the impact of the oil embargo, and the letter was meant to allay their apprehensions and offer an apologia.

". . . The United States has compromised its own stated foreign policy by continuing to support Israel's military expansion," said the letter which was signed by a Christian clergyman who is AMEU's chief executive. "This departure from even-handedness in the Middle East has alienated our traditional allies among the Arabs." The embargo, the letter added, has been imposed by the Arabs as "something of a last resort."

There was an enclosure with the letter to the truckers. It was a leaflet produced by the Arab Information Center. Entitled "More in Sorrow than in Anger—the Arab Case for Oil and Justice," it was also sent by Americans for Middle East Understanding to a selected list of service station owners in the fuel-short Midwest. The recipients may possibly have been aware of the fact that Americans for Middle East Understanding is a tax-exempt organization which has been funded mainly by the Aramco consortium (i.e., Exxon, Mobil, Texaco and SoCal) and which has received contributions as well from Continental, Ashland and Mara-

172

thon Oil. But there was nothing in the mailing piece to indicate that the Arab Information Center's contribution, that leaflet about oil and justice, was part of a giant conspiracy against Israel.

It is impossible to separate the network of the Arab Information Center from this conspiracy. The Center's parent body, the Arab League, helped engineer the oil embargo. The League's decision-makers are also the rulers of the Arab states which are waging the war against Israel. They are the sponsors of the PLO, whose leaders now sit as equals in League councils. And just as the regional boycott offices are adjuncts of a central, League-sponsored body dealing with the economic war against Israel, so the Arab Information Center offices are blocks in the pyramid whose upper levels are occupied by the leaders among the Arab belligerents.

At the top is the Council of Arab Information Ministers, made up of cabinet-rank officials of member states. They meet annually to plan and coordinate strategy, basing their decisions on the ever-changing shifts and balances of the total war effort. (The decision to sell the concept of a mini-state in Palestine was taken after the member nations voted at a summit to recognize the PLO as the "sole representative" of the Palestinians. Such decision-making is described by a prestigious Egyptian magazine as "examining trends in Israeli propaganda and developing means to counter it." This is untrue: what the Arabs do rarely has anything to do with what the Israelis do.)

Next is the permanent Committee for Arab Information, composed of the directors of the information networks of the various Arab states. This committee drafts the master plans for the world-wide propaganda drives.

Subordinate to the Committee for Arab Information is the Office for Arab Information. It is a permanent body composed of the press attachés of the Arab embassies in Cairo. This office oversees the activities of the information network outside the confines of the Arab world.

Next is the Information Administration, which serves as the "connecting link" abroad and maintains "special offices" for planning, coordination, research and "control." These special offices include the outposts of the Arab Information Center.

In addition to its massive operation in the United States, the Arab League operates out of Geneva, Rome, Bonn, London, Paris, Ottawa, New Delhi, Tokyo, Buenos Aires, Rio de Janeiro and Dakar. The expressed task of its "information" network is to expose "the lies and deceit which are the foundation of Zionist and Israeli propaganda," and to establish "organized contact with groups which can pressure and influence the decision-makers in various countries."

There are a great many groups the Arabs can use to "pressure and influence the decision-makers" in a country like the United States, where lobbying is an accepted method of political action. The use, however, by Big Oil of propaganda processed by the Arab belligerents has gone largely unnoticed. Few stockholders and few, if any, holders of oil company credit-cards know that their investments and the tanks of gas they buy may help finance the circulation of foreign propaganda aimed against Israel through tax-exempt foundations.

According to *Time* Magazine, American oil companies spent $9 million sponsoring pro-Arab groups between 1967 and 1975. *Time* failed to mention that some of these groups maintain close relationships with the Arab Information Center and act to distribute propaganda calling for the elimination of Israel.

There is a certain amount of overlap between two very

active organizations with oil funding—the aforementioned
Americans for Middle East Understanding and Americans
for Near East Refugee Aid. Like Americans for Middle
East Understanding, Americans for Near East Refugee Aid
is tax-exempt because of its "non-profit, philanthropic"
status. Like AMEU, it has received large contributions
from the Aramco companies. Americans for Near East Refugee Aid received a whopping $2.2 million gift from Gulf
Oil just six days after the Arabs cut back crude oil production and tied the resumption of full production to cessation
of U.S. support for Israel. There was, Gulf's Public Relations Director later solemnly told a Senate Investigating
Subcommittee, absolutely no connection between the do-
nation and the fact that 75 per cent of Gulf's crude oil reserves are in Kuwait.

(Soon after that generous gift was made, Gulf contribut-
ed $50 thousand for a mysterious educational program to
promote "understanding" of the Arab cause in the U.S.
and funneled the money through the First National City
Bank in Beirut, a "laundering" operation designed to hide
the transaction. It was an awkward way to finance a U.S.-
based program, but Gulf said that is what they were asked
to do.)

There are some peculiarly fascinating intersections in
this particular world. For example, the summer, 1976, issue
of the newsletter of Americans for Middle East Understanding carried extracts from a speech before the American Arab Chamber of Commerce and Industry in New
York by the Saudi Minister of Industry, who said that the
Arab boycott did not represent racial or religious discrimination and that its sole purpose was "to prohibit transactions with any enterprise which fosters the economy of
Israel." The newsletter's front page was devoted to a re-
print of a speech delivered at a symposium, held at the

Washington Islamic Center on February 5, 1976, by Dr. John H. Davis, who has been a member of the board of Americans for Middle East Understanding since 1967. In that speech, Dr. Davis said:

. . . Because the motivation for America to do business with the Arab people is a compliment [*sic*] of her purchase of Arab oil, the need for this is just as great as is U.S. need for oil.

America's interest in Israel's survival is of a different order. It is an interest based entirely on a commitment, rather than a need. In fact, the commitment for Israel's survival runs directly counter to America's self-interest in that it makes difficult the procurement of Arab oil and the doing of business with Arab states and people. . . . The most logical thing for the United States to do would be to compromise Israel's existence. For, while the U.S. could survive well without Israel, she cannot survive well at all without both Arab oil and Arab business. . . . In December, 1975, the issue of Jewish exclusiveness in Israel did come before the United Nations General Assembly in the form of the resolution that described Zionism as racism. . . . Zionism in its support of Jewish exclusivism is inherently racist, of this there can be no doubt.

It is my belief that Israel cannot permanently exist as a state if she insists on being a Jewish state for the Jewish people. . . . Certain Palestinian groups have opposed the creation of a Palestinian state consisting of the West Bank and the Gaza Strip because they want Israel to become part of a secular Palestine now. It is my belief that, if the Palestinian Arabs did accept a mini-state consisting of the West Bank and the Gaza Strip . . . in time (less than twenty years) Israel would be forced to abandon the concept of Jewish exclusivism and become a secular state, even part of a large secular state. This would be so because a small exclusivist state based on the Law of the Return could not remain viable in the Middle East. The forces militating against the survival of such an exclusivist state would be too over-powering.

Dr. Davis was not only a member of the board of Americans for Middle East Understanding, which is financed largely by American oil money. He was also the chairman of Americans for Near East Refugee Aid, financed in part by American oil money.

The publication which printed his speech is called, in wholly unconscious irony, *The Link*.

Georgetown University.
Location: Washington, D.C. 20057.
Campus: Urban outskirts.
Undergraduate Enrollment: 2900 M. 2600 W.
Total Enrollment: 10,715.
Expenses: $5,500.
Financial Aid: 20%.

The first operative fact was that figure for financial aid, quoted in the annual college guide of the *Yale Daily News*. At Stanford, 43 per cent of the student body received financial aid. At Princeton, the figure was 42 per cent; at Harvard, 65 per cent. Those three universities, like Georgetown, are traditional stepping stones to a career in government. But there was a difference. The *Yale Guide* called it "red ink." Georgetown University needed money badly. Under the name of "Impact '81," the administrators and trustees of the Catholic university launched a drive in the mid-1970s to raise $51 million for endowed chairs, increased financial aid to needy students and such necessities as a swimming pool.

The second operative fact was Georgetown's peculiar status in the Nation's capital. On this point, the *Yale Guide*

177

said: ". . . it's the place to be, academically and probably socially, in Washington."

In 1976, the United Arab Emirates, the Sultanate of Oman, the Arab Republic of Egypt and Mobil Oil presented Georgetown University with $275 thousand. But there were strings attached: the money was to be used to set up a center for the study of Contemporary Arab Society. The center was to be attached to the School of Foreign Service, a training center for future U.S. diplomats.

There is a staggering amount of Arab money looking for useful investments of this nature around the powerful city of Washington, so much money, in fact, that people with suspicious minds started to examine gifts in their own neighborhoods. As a result, a bill was introduced in the Virginia Assembly by four legislators who were concerned about a $625 thousand Saudi Arabian donation to a Virginia elementary school. The bill would have restricted foreign gifts to public bodies and institutions in the state to $50 thousand; it died in committee.

The Terraset School is not simply a Virginia public school. It is the elementary school which serves the "New Town" of Reston, an innovative community near Washington. The Reston Homeowners' Association is the official governing body of the town. The majority of its votes belong to Gulf Reston, a company formed when Gulf Oil bought out the original builders. The school system is part of the Fairfax County complex of public schools.

Late in November, 1974, Reston's residents were disappointed to learn that the federal government had decided not to finance the solar heating plant which would have made Terraset the first public school heated by sunlight in the U.S. Soon afterward, the Saudi government approached Fairfax County with an offer to foot the bill for the solar plant. The Saudi representatives claimed that they had heard of the school's need through a "consultant." So interested were the Saudis in Terraset's heating system that a Saudi prince filled out a personal check for $150 thousand to keep the work going while the rest of the money cleared the bank.

"Tell them not to put away their checkbooks," said a member of the Virginia Assembly when the bill to limit such benefactions came up in committee. "I have a lot more schools in Virginia that need the money."

The Saudis explained their interest in Terraset as purely scientific, claiming that it costs less money to build a working plant in the United States than to mount such a project in sunny Riyadh. They were, they said, interested in solar heat as a means of stretching their oil resources. One of the Virginia delegates who introduced the short-lived bill had little patience with such arguments.

"I am under no illusions whatsoever that they are interested in solar energy," said Ira Lechner (D-Arlington). "No matter what they say, they want the world to be dependent on oil, not solar energy. This is the very beginning of a long-range public relations battle and it is the beginning of a very sophisticated campaign. They were attempting to make friends in Reston, where the sons and daughters of many government officials go to school. And sooner or later, something will be asked and something given."

Lechner, a man of some stature in the legislature, called the matter of the Saudi Arabian gift "The Tale of Terraset, or The Best Things in Life Are Free." His plea to the Virginia Assembly, he said, was based on "an old Virginia tradition" which has sometimes shown itself in rejection even of federal funds in instances that impinged on the independence of the state.

179

"I have never yet heard of a giv-ee saying to a giver, 'Go to hell,'" Lechner said. "And that is embodied in a universal principle established since the first apple."

Those were words for Georgetown University to ponder. In Washington, the links between benefaction, power, oil and Arabs can be tight links.

The Middle East Institute in Washington maintains an aura of scholarship and neutrality. The Institute supports an excellent library at its dignified town-house headquarters on N Street.

The Institute's board of governors is heavy with Arabists, men who have spent their careers in the Arab world and admire Arab culture and the Arab way of life. The board membership includes an ex-envoy to Saudi Arabia, three former ambassadors to Egypt, a former ambassador to Jordan—but no former envoys to another Middle Eastern country: Israel.

The former ambassador to Jordan is a retired diplomat named L. Dean Brown. Brown was Gerald Ford's choice when the administration decided to send an experienced man to Beirut to mediate between the Moslem and Christian belligerents. His mission failed and he returned in May, 1976, with some remarkable views. "He paid tribute," a *New York Times* interviewer reported, "to . . . the Syrian armed forces for 'playing a helpful role' in establishing a neutral zone in Beirut, and the Palestinians 'for playing a calming role' with the Lebanese Moslem allies."

On the same page *The Times* carried an AP dispatch from Beirut reporting that more than seventy persons were killed and 150 wounded in the Lebanese capital in the preceding twenty-four hours. Efforts by the combatant leaders to meet and talk truce were frustrated because "the no-man's-land between the two sides was under heavy shelling.''

And what of his mission of mediation? Brown said he did not think there would be real peace in Lebanon '' 'until there is a Palestinian state' that would distract the Palestinian guerrillas from their present involvement in Lebanese politics.''

Brown did not mention any fears of a possible involvement on the part of Palestinians with the internal politics of Israel. He did, however, tell a meeting after his return that Israel was a "non-viable" state. Questioned about that striking statement by a member of the audience, Brown explained that he meant non-viable in economic terms.

L. Dean Brown was concurrently the head of the Middle East Institute. The Institute received nearly half its operating budget in 1974 from oil companies vitally interested in supporting the Arabs.

11

Sadat and the Big Lie

Nasser: Will we say the U.S. and England or just the U.S.?

Hussein: The U.S. and England.

Nasser: Does Britain have aircraft carriers?

Hussein: (Answer unintelligible).

Nasser: By Allah, I say that I will make an announcement and you will make an announcement and we will see to it that the Syrians make an announcement that American and British airplanes are taking part against us from aircraft carriers. We will stress the matter and we will drive the point home.

(Conversation between Gamal Abdel Nasser of Egypt and King Hussein of Jordan, recorded by an Israeli radio ham in June, 1967, in which the two leaders determined to blame their defeat of the Six-Day War on a wholly fictitious air-strike by England and America.)

". . . The important thing is that the United States began to enter the battle through an air bridge they set up

183

quickly. The Americans began to send aircraft and pilots and tanks with their crews. All this landed at el 'Arish airfield and was moved immediately to the battlefield. From 17 October I was fighting against the United States and U.S. arms and equipment. This would not have been possible to continue without risking the lives of my sons, heroic fighters who are to me the most precious elements of honorable fighting. . . ."

(Anwar el-Sadat on Cairo Radio, Oct. 29, 1975, blaming his defeats in the later stages of the 1973 war on a wholly fictitious armed intervention by the United States, as recorded and transcribed by the U.S. Foreign Broadcast Information Service.)

More than years separate those two fictions. The first was launched when relations between the Arabs and the West were at low ebb and Egypt had broken off diplomatic relations with the countries chosen as scapegoats. There were no efforts to shield Nasser and Hussein from the derision which followed publication of the exchange in Western capitals. In Washington and London, it was instantly branded as a lie.

By the time Anwar el-Sadat launched his greater lie, attitudes in the West had undergone a change. In 1975, oil was king. Sadat was now an ally and, in the view of the State Department, a man of moderation to be shielded from embarrassment. Thus, although the quotations used in this chapter depend entirely on the U.S. government's own listening service, there are very few Americans who know that Sadat was permitted to get away with a lengthy series of such libels against the United States, the last of them broadcast after he had already left Egypt for a state visit to Washington.

The decision to introduce a second fictitious American intervention into the history of the unending war against Israel came a full eighteen months after the "fact." By that time, Egypt had already been paid in full for her ostensible swing away from the Soviet Union and her new friendship with the United States. Through the good offices of the Ford Administration, with Henry Kissinger acting as broker, Sadat had been handed the fruits of the victory he had failed to win in the field: the Abu Rodeis oil fields, two strategic Sinai passes and full access to the Suez Canal, all prizes which Israel had wrested from Egypt in the preemptive strike known as the Six-Day War. In return, Sadat had given very little: he had agreed to tone down (but not to halt) his vicious propaganda campaign against Israel; he had agreed to permit ships (but not ships of Israeli registry) to carry certain cargoes bound for Israel through the Suez; and he had agreed to two stages of "disengagement" in the Sinai and had signed a pledge of truce (but no pledge of non-belligerency).

The respect with which Sadat viewed his own concessions was minimal. He hastened, even before he began the planting of his big lie, to assure the Arabs at large of his unwavering intent to go on as he always has.

". . . When it was decided to repatriate the refugees to the towns of the Canal," he told an "information convention" on February 2, 1975, speaking of a project which would require copious American aid, "the quibblers said it meant that Egypt would not fight again; now this is really funny. . . ."

"Who said that the preparations for war contradict continuing construction?" he asked an interviewer for *Ros el-Youssef* later that year. "We have long ago adopted the motto: 'One hand to work, and the other to arms.'"

But such threatening innuendo was no longer enough to appease Sadat's jealous critics. In early summer of 1975, just as he was planning his triumphant American tour with its enormous economic and military value to Egypt, the

Arab alliance which had planned and executed the Yom Kippur War began to come apart at the seams. Sadat's battle companion, Hafez al-Assad, joined the leaders of Algeria and Libya to denounce the imminent signing of the second "disengagement" with Israel which would give Sadat the Sinai passes and oil fields. With the PLO, they accused Sadat of self-serving gluttony in his acceptance of territorial concessions which left the rest of the big losers out in the cold. He was charged as being a "traitor" because of his agreement to a truce which, it was alleged, would remove Egypt from confrontation with Israel. Worst of all, there were nasty cracks from Assad and Qaddafi about Sadat's conduct of the 1973 war.

Sadat was hard put to defend himself on the war record. Although he was able to interpret the territorial concessions as prizes of battle, they really had nothing to do with the battle situation at war's end. In fact, the Yom Kippur War had concluded with the bulk of Sadat's tanks in the Sinai destroyed, Suez City under siege and Israeli armor deployed on the Egyptian side of the Canal within striking distance of Cairo itself. It was humiliating to be reminded that the Israelis had vaulted into Egypt from the Sinai bank of the Canal and had held 30-40,000 men of the Egyptian Third Army in a death grip, cut off from food, water and aid for their many wounded. It was humiliating to be reminded that American pressure on the infuriated Israelis, coupled with Soviet threats, had been required to bring about a firm cease-fire and to save the best of Egypt's armies.

By the time his erstwhile Arab allies turned on him, Sadat had used the happy ending of his war to sanctify the venture in several guises, with himself cast in a role as glorious as Saladin's. The first casualty of truth was the link between the initial attack and the fact that the war had deliberately been launched on Yom Kippur when, the Arabs knew, the Israelis would be most vulnerable. In the Arab world, the Yom Kippur War does not exist; that term holds uncomfortable connotations of deceit, unworthy of brave warriors, on a day of consummate holiness to the Jews. In its stead, there are two other wars: the October War and the Ramadan War.

The very word *October* has come to take on almost magical meaning among Arabs. The October War is linked with a new term for *jihad* (the "October Spirit") and for armed training (the "October Brigades") and, in Hafez al-Assad's words, "the October memories."

On October 6, 1975, the second anniversary of the war, Assad described the day of the attacks as one of "holiness, dignity or greatness" and went on to tell students at Damascus University:

> The 6th of October—the 10th day of Ramadan—is a day in which the greatest event happened in the history of the area and in which one of the greatest historic events in the world took place. On this day, the 6th of October, the Arab appeared as he really is—courageous and strong and capable of overcoming the difficulties he encounters and cr h-ing the challenges facing him—an Arab who hates and refuses to live in humiliation and adores death with honor, an Arab who, when faced by mountains, seeks to climb to the top and from the top looks with compassion and generosity to those on the ground who were incapable climbing to the top mountain. [*applause*]
>
> In October, the Arab human being emerged in his true image. Looking at the sky, he sees it close to his forehead. Looking at the land, the soil of homeland on which he lives, he seeks the blood of his fathers and forefathers. . . .

In addition to such celebrations of the anniversary of the initial attack, Arab countries go on to add festivity and

187

speech-making to commemorate the duration of the *entire campaign*. For Anwar el-Sadat denies that his Third Army was ever encircled or his capital threatened. And he celebrates the last, desperate days along the Canal, before the Great Powers stepped in to save him, as "the Glorious Battle Of Suez" with religious observances.

The second Yom Kippur War, the Ramadan War, is an invention which has found wide acceptance in other Arab countries. It has its genealogy in the juxtaposition, on October 6, 1973, of Yom Kippur and the tenth day of the holy month of Ramadan, which Moslems mark each year with daily fasts and which culminates in the feast of 'Id el-Fit'r. If October had less unpleasant connotations than Yom Kippur, Ramadan was better than either, and Sadat wasted no time in incorporating his war with the Jews into Islamic observance. In this, he was aided by a controlled press and by such ventures as the publication of Mohammed Hassenein Heikal's history of the war, *The Road to Ramadan*. Sadat turned the city of Suez into a site of pilgrimate for 'Id el-Fit'r. He continued to memorialize the Islamic dates of the 1973 war in symbolic acts such as the laying of cornerstones along the Canal during subsequent Ramadans. His civic acts were echoed in prayers throughout the Arab world. The only problem, if it can be called a problem, is that Sadat had, between October and Ramadan, too much of a good thing.

For the Moslem calendar of which Ramadan is an entire month is based on an uncorrected lunar progression which lags further and further behind the Gregorian calendar by eleven days in each succeeding year. It will not be until the year 2009 that the Ramadan and October dates will come together again. By 1975, when Sadat found it necessary to alter the history of the war still further, Ramadan had already slipped back to September, but the Egyptian Chief of

Staff demonstratively inaugurated the holy month by visiting troops in the Canal cities of Port Said, Ismailia and Suez, and Sadat himself went to Suez City on 'Id el-Fit'r.

Although he had enshrined himself in Islamic religious observance, Sadat held doggedly to his secular role of victor. He had failed to satisfy his critics with assurances of his bellicosity in the confrontation with Israel and he had to find another way. He chose Nasser's way. But Sadat was no Nasser. A wilier man, he had no desire to court the ridicule of the West or jeopardize his profitable new relationship with the United States. Instead, he chose to develop his big lie in easy stages, using Egyptian parliamentary sessions, Arab Socialist Union meetings and selected interviews for maximum effect. It was a slow intravenous drip rather than Nasser's radical surgery, but it succeeded masterfully. The Arab world loves nothing so much as "evidence" of American imperialist venture. And at no time did the scapegoat choose even to acknowledge the libels Sadat unfolded over the next months, much less deny the presence of an American fighting force on Israeli-held Arab territory. Rather than clear its sullied name, the United States chose silence. There was enough trouble involved in the then forthcoming struggle to convince the American public, traumatized by Vietnam, to sanction the dispatch of two hundred *unarmed* technicians to man the Sinai Early Warning System which was part of the complex six-point deal required to get Egypt to agree to truce.

The events which formed the backdrop to Sadat's fiction had their beginnings with the war's outbreak and ended on January 18, 1974, with the implementation of the first Israeli-Egyptian disengagement agreement.

On October 6, massive Egyptian forces poured eastward across the Suez into Sinai and almost the entire Syrian army struck across the Golan Heights. The Arabs had the aggressor's initial advantage, the Israelis having abandoned the thought of a pre-emptive strike to please world opinion. The Israeli gesture was soon forgotten. Secretary of State Kissinger, quickly concluding that a decisive Israeli victory would simply restore an imbalance of power and inhibit progress toward negotiated settlement, decided that the war must produce, in the words of an authorized historian, "neither victor nor vanquished." Disregarding appeals from Jerusalem, Kissinger deliberately stalled on shipments of weaponry to Israel.

On October 13, President Nixon, reacting finally to a massive and immediate Soviet arms lift to Damascus and Cairo, countermanded Kissinger, and an American air re-supply to Israel began. On the northern front, Israel by then had broken the Syrian attack and begun a slow advance toward Damascus. The Egyptians, however, had over-whelmed the thinly held Bar Lev defense line along the Suez and built up their tank forces in the Sinai.

On October 15, in the war's turning point, an Israeli armored column knifed through the invading Egyptians, crossed the canal into Egypt and swept southward toward the Gulf of Suez, sending a secondary column north toward Ismailia. The Russians, alarmed by reports from their spy satellites, warned Sadat that the Israeli attack was not camouflage or a feint but a serious thrust which could im-peril his Sinai armies and threaten Cairo itself, but even Premier Kosygin, visiting the capital, could not shake Sadat's stubborn confidence. With Kosygin back in Moscow with the news, Brezhnev virtually summoned Kissinger to an emergency conference. There, despite pledges to the Is-raelis that he would temporize to provide them with time to complete their victory, Kissinger speedily agreed to an im-posed cease-fire "in place."

On October 22, the cease-fire took effect but, by then, the southern column of the Israeli invasion force had swept almost to the Gulf of Suez, virtually closing all supply routes to the besieged Third Army in the Sinai, and was within easy reach of Suez City, while the northern column was on the outskirts of Ismailia, halfway up the Canal. Desperate Egyptian bursts of fire soon broke the UN truce and Israeli units, taking advantage of the excuse this gave them, surrounded Suez City and sprang the trap on the 30-40,000 men of the Third Army before a second cease-fire went into effect on October 24.

Moscow again displayed concern and Kissinger—who was determined that the war end in military impasse and that Israeli bargaining power be neutralized—used Soviet threats to good effect and compelled an infuriated Israel to open a supply corridor to the Third Army.

Two weeks later, Kissinger flew off to Cairo in pursuit of the détente with Sadat which was to result in the renewal of diplomatic relations.

On January 18, a disengagement accord, brokered by Kissinger, was signed. It provided for withdrawal of the Israeli force from the Egyptian side of the Canal, releasing the Third Army from its long state of siege.

At no time in the entire period covered by Sadat's lies did the U.S. ever intervene militarily in the conflict. There were no American pilots, no American tank crews, no U.S. troops in the field. The U.S. spy satellite, whose reports Sadat so resented, was matched by Soviet spy rigs of equal efficiency. There was no U.S. base on Egyptian territory, occupied or otherwise, and the U.S. airlift to Israel did not use El 'Arish airport as its staging ground: the gigantic Galaxies which carried the American resupply—big as these planes were, the matériel they carried totaled one-tenth the

191

tonnage the Kremlin rushed to the Arabs—thundered low over Tel Aviv and made their landings at nearby Ben Gurion airport.

But Henry Kissinger had erred in one crucial area. He was following the advice of people who had, for years, believed the Arabs when they swore they would deal reasonably with Israel when parity was restored. In fact, where Sadat was concerned, there could be no parity and no possibility of a war without a victor. Snatched from the very brink of disaster, he had no gratitude for his rescuers. He was to refer contemptuously to the Israeli salient which threatened all Egypt as a "pocket," a "gap between two armies," a "pass." He was to call the offensive which might have swept on to Cairo or up the Canal to Port Said a "television battle" of no military substance. Out of his salvaged pride, he was to fabricate a great victory in which he was a wholly heroic figure and, in so doing, he was to libel the United States again and again. He began slowly, but Radio Cairo was there and he was heard by millions of Egyptians, and his first forum was the Egyptian parliament. His message to a joint session of the People's National Assembly and the Arab Socialist Union on September 5, 1975, exactly one day after the formal signing of the American backed second disengagement, was one of victory:

> . . . Put simply, as I stated at the last ASU National Congress, if the supreme Arab interest demands that we make peace, we shall make peace. If that supreme interest demands that we negotiate, we shall negotiate. If that supreme interest demands that we fight, we shall fight.
> We fought, we negotiated, and we triumphed. [*applause*]
> We fought in 1973 and defeated Israel. We confronted the United States itself on the battlefield for more than ten days. Yes, we confronted the United States when it rushed to

save Israel and began to send weapons and technicians directly to Sinai, directly behind the battleline.

Despite this, we consolidated our positions east of the Suez Canal. When the fighting stopped, all of the Bar-Lev Line was in our hands. When the fighting stopped, we had achieved one of the very important aims we had taken into our calculations in planning the battle. We emerged from the battle with 90 per cent of our armed forces completely intact. [*applause*]

Sadat went further on September 15 in an address to the Secretariat General of the Arab Socialist Union. Again, it was broadcast live. He spoke of Kosygin's warnings of danger from the Israeli canal crossing:

. . . The lines were breached while Kosygin was here. He tried to use this to exert pressure on me. I told him this [the Egyptian campaign] was not a theoretical battle; five [Egyptian] divisions were on the east [Sinai] bank and not one man would be withdrawn, and that my tanks were on the East bank and I would be dealing with [the Israeli invasion force on] the West bank. Talk about the Israelis being on the way to Cairo was sheer nonsense. When the Soviet Premier left, I was still refusing to call a cease-fire. This was the situation until 19 October.

. . . By that night in particular, I had been confronting the United States for ten days. The United States took up a base at El 'Arish so that they would reach the front in the shortest possible time. Of course, everything was at the service of Israel. After that, I learned that a U.S. satellite was taking pictures daily. When one of our armored divisions moved from West to East [to Sinai] in response to Syria's request for us to step up our military action along our front to ease pressure on Syria, the Americans photographed this and passed it on to the Israelis. The operation to open up the breach [the Israeli armored thrust across the Suez] was planned at that time. . . .

By the 19th I found myself fighting the United States for ten days on the battlefield. The United States threw in all its weight. . . .

Such was the situation on 19 October when the United States had a base on my territory, and with the Soviet Union pressing me [to accept a cease-fire before Egypt's military situation grew desperate]. I had to make a decision.

The first thing I did [on the 19th] was send a message at 0200 to President Hafez al-Assad in Syria. In the message I explained the situation to him and told him I had made a decision right then for a cease-fire because I was not [agreeable to] fighting America. I said I was prepared to account for this decision before my own people and before the entire Arab nation, but I was not prepared to sacrifice my people, my soil or the Egyptian army as actually happened [in the Six-Day War] in 1967. . . . [applause]

From this point on, we start a strange new phase that has the effect of shedding light on today's stands and on the deliberate misinformation put in front of the Arab man in the street. You know what happened after the cease-fire. . . . The Syrian Ba'ath Party then told the Arab nation that it was Sadat who asked for a cease-fire and lost the battle of the Arabs and that Syria was preparing a counter-offensive and that Syria was continuing the battle.

. . . The Arab nation was told that it was Sadat who asked for a cease-fire; it was Egypt which halted the battle—I who stood alone confronting the United States for ten days and in spite of the fact that it was the United States, I halted [the fighting] at [the] line [of October] 22, which was fatal for Israel by their [own] admission. . . .

It has been proved that I sent him [Assad] a cable on the 19th, three days before [the cease-fire], explaining the matter to him and telling him that I agreed to the cease-fire with my heart bleeding because I was not prepared to shoulder historically the responsibility of destroying Egypt's armed forces again and sacrifice my sons and people once more. I was fighting the United States and I am not equal to it. I am not one of those who boasts of one-up-manship; I do not fight the United States. I fight Israel, not the United States. . . .

Five weeks later, in the midst of the celebrations of the second anniversary of the glorious Ramadan victory, the Middle East News Agency broadcast—in Arabic—the contents of an interview in which Sadat (not for the first time) blamed the growth of that Israeli "salient" on an incompetent Chief of Staff and explained that this was the reason he had dismissed the general. Sadat referred, in an interview with the Board Chairman of a powerful Egyptian daily, to "that day of the October war which is dearest" to his heart, and it was, astonishingly, October 19. On that day, the Sadat story went, the Commander of the Egyptian forces decided to carry out an action to block the corridor through which the Israeli tanks were passing "in increasing numbers" to the Egyptian side of the Suez.

"When," Sadat continued, "I heard the report of the [Egyptian] commandos' seizure of . . . the entrance to the salient—and that they were in control and determined to block the salient completely, I felt the greatness of our heroic fighters and I was proud of this courageous spirit of self-sacrifice. However, the Chief of Staff who was charged with the elimination of the salient ordered the commandos to withdraw so he could complete the gathering of information. . . . For this reason I dimissed him. . . ."

A few days after that interview, Sadat was back on course, with the United States as scapegoat. He finished the job. The occasion was the anniversary of the final battle of the October war, the battle in which the Israeli "salient" grew to reach the Gulf of Suez and surround Suez City. By the time the following question-and-answer session was broadcast to the Arab world via Radio Cairo, on October 29, 1975, Sadat was en route to the United States on his visit of friendship:

Q. Your excellency, Mr. President: I convey to you the people's congratulations on the anniversary of the immortal battle of Suez. I hope you will give the citizens a picture of the circumstances of the Suez battle of 24 October, 1973, since you issued your historic order to defend Suez to the last man, woman and child, and will describe the significance of Egyptian steadfastness on that day—of the Egyptian who recovered his feeling of full freedom.

A. In the name of God. In fact, this subject raises beautiful memories, because you might have noticed that in the past years, on the past two feasts of 'Id el-Fit'r, I prayed in Suez, and I have made it a rule that the 'Id el-Fit'r prayers are relayed [by radio] from Suez. I remember that, following the [first] cease-fire I went to the command at the moment when the firing ceased, that is at 1900 on 22 October. I was in the operations room with all the commanders, just as I was with them precisely when the operations began on 6 October. From our actual experience with the Israeli enemy it becomes clear that he always exploits the cease-fire to try to improve his position. . . . The firing ceased and two hours later, as is the wont of the Jews, they issued a statement saying that Egypt violated the cease-fire, moved its forces and so on because they were in a dilemma. Indeed, Israel was following the myth of the unbeatable Israeli Army. They achieved a breakthrough on the southern side. They also made an attempt on the northern side toward Ismailia, but the concentration was on the south. They seized the opportunity following the cease-fire and broke through. . . .

The interview then shifted to a somewhat less delicate subject. The questioner asked: "Your excellency, did you expect the armed force to attain all that was attained heroically on the soil of Sinai?"

A. I was optimistic about victory. We prepared well-studied scientific plans for the battle, covering all details, duties and tasks. . . . Every commander and every fighter knew his duties, was trained in them. . . . I was, therefore, optimistic and reassured. My sons, members of the armed forces, were in the highest state of preparedness and alert. At the same time, I was aware of my sons, members of our good people. I know them to be noble men and heroes during times of hardship. I also took into consideration the fact that sons of the entire Arab nation were eagerly looking forward to the battle of honor, dignity and pride, and that a battle would enflame them and bring out all their potentialities and zeal. . . .

I had planned the battle to last as long as possible. The late King Feisal [of Saudi Arabia] agreed with me on this. His Majesty asked me to make the battle last as long as possible so that the Arab public would have time to form an opinion.

Q. Will you permit me to ask whether the October War achieved its aim as planned?

A. We attained our aims in half a battle, though we had calculated to attain these aims in a complete battle. When the first news of the war reached the United States . . . Tel Aviv then contacted the United States to say: "We will crush the enemy within two days and will teach him a lesson he will never forget." After two days, Israel contacted the United States to say: "We have spent the past two days in preparation in view of the Day of Atonement and the season of holidays." The American officials asked: "Are you in need of any arms or equipment?" The Israelis replied: "We have all that we need right now. We will require replacements for our losses in the future."

The two days passed but they could not crush our bones. They were defeated and withdrew in panic. Dayan broke down in the battlefield and wept in front of the foreign and Israeli pressmen, because he was sure that he had lost the war. He said: "We will never be able to make the Egyptians budge an inch." Hence the message: Save Israel. This message was carried by the Israeli Ambassador in Washington. Therefore, Kissinger once again contacted Golda Meir, who admitted that the situation was critical. Kissinger, with his strategic mind, realized that Israel had lost this round. Thus he asked the Pentagon to take measures to save Israel. The American satellite thus began to get a picture of the situation, and on the basis of this picture, the extent and volume of American aid should be determined.

Q. Then satellites did not take pictures of the first four days?

A. They only photographed the situation after the fourth day.

Q. What a pity. They would have recorded for history glittering pictures of one of the most important stages of development of our war with the enemy.

A. The impression of the Israeli commanders was that the fighting was no more than an Arab whim which Israel would firmly and cruelly force the Arabs to retract. Thus [at first] nobody paid any attention to record the fighting. They failed to grasp the truth about it, as shown by Israel's official reports.

The important thing is that the United States began to enter the battle through an air bridge they set up quickly. The Americans began to send aircraft and pilots and tanks with their crews. All this landed at el-'Arish airfield and was moved immediately to the battlefield. From 17 October I was fighting against the United States and U.S. arms and equipment. This would not have been possible to continue without risking the lives of my sons, heroic fighters who are to me the most precious elements of honorable fighting.

But America's intervention on the side of Israel created a new situation and consequently led to a new American position and to the first disengagement of forces and then to the second disengagement of forces when our aims of battle, which were to reach the [Sinai] passes, were achieved. We had only carried out half the battle plan. They [the Americans] were then the ones who cut our battle in half. But half the battle achieved the aims of the entire battle.

Q. What if the United States had not intervened?

A. We would have continued our battle until the passes and the oilfields and then the rest of the Sinai came within our grasp, to be taken whenever we wanted.

Q. . . . But there were fears that the [Israeli] forces in the gap [across the Suez] in Egypt might spread into the depths of the valley and into Cairo itself, for example.

A. Would they have dared to enter Cairo? . . . I never imagined, not for one single moment, that this would have been possible or that their madness would drive them to this extent. The gap was only a television battle exploited for propaganda more than it was a military action to be reckoned with. We had drawn up a plan [after the October 24 cease-fire] to destroy the gap and liquidate it completely. But Kissinger told me that, had this taken place, the United States would have entered the war against us openly and clearly. This alone is enough proof that the gap was an American plan to save the face of Israel before the world and nothing more, to be used later as some sort of overt propaganda. . . .

Several days after that interview was broadcast in Arabic, Anwar el-Sadat was in Chicago, where he was warmly welcomed by Mayor Daley, who referred to him flatteringly as a moderate man. Sadat's reply:

. . . Mr. Mayor, Friends: I am confident that you are aware that we spare no efforts to work for the realization of a just and durable peace in the Middle East. We do so for the welfare of the people of the area and for the sake of peace and stability in the world. The United States has

199

helped us in the process of achieving peace. We have reason to believe that this role will continue in the future. Such a stand by the United States will undoubtedly further the expansion of the ties of friendship and cooperation between our two peoples and countries. . . .

Soon afterward, an American interviewer courteously inquired of Sadat how he could assure that the arms he had requested of the United States would be used, as he claimed, for defensive purposes. In reply, Sadat cited three guarantors: "My attitude toward peace, the steps I have already taken, and the validity of my word."

12

*A*rms

Between 1973 and 1975, U.S. arms sales to Kuwait rose from $53,000 to $350,000,000.

In the same period, U.S. arms sales to Saudi Arabia went up from $161,000,000 to more than $2 billion.

Syria gathered more—many more—surface-to-air missiles than any single European NATO power. So did Egypt. Saudi Arabia received $4 billion in U.S. weaponry and military construction in a matter of months. And two years after the Yom Kippur War, the combined arms budgets of the Arab states dedicated to the military eradication of Israel totalled $16 billion.

Israel's latest armaments budget, according to the reliable International Institute for Strategic Studies, was $3.5 billion.

The mad binge of arms buying in the Middle East has brought some of the most underdeveloped countries in the world to a staggeringly sophisticated level of destructive capacity. The Arabs today have virtually every weapon possessed by the big powers except for strategic missiles and nuclear warheads. Commanding only 2 per cent of the world's gross national product, they are, in comparative economic terms, the most heavily militarized countries in the world.

They consider weapons more important by far than any social need of their peoples. In 1973, before the latest speed-up of arms buying, Egypt was spending $48 per capita on weapons as against $11 per capita on education and $6 on health. Syria spent $56 per capita on arms, $14 on education and $2 on health. Saudi Arabia spent $139 per capita on weapons, $56 on education and $15 on health. No later figures were available, but it was perfectly obvious that the ratios were growing more lop-sided by the month.

The arms build-up in the Middle East is not simply, as it is often called, a "race" between the Israelis and the Arabs. It is an infinitely complex series of interlocking competitions between Arabs and Jews, Arabs and Arabs, Arab and non-Arab Moslems, East and West. Its Arab participants include: the Confrontation States—Egypt, Syria, Jordan and Lebanon; Libya to the west and Iraq to the east of the front lines; the jingoistic countries farther to the east, in the area the Shah of Iran calls the Persian Gulf and the Saudis call the Arabian Gulf; second-string countries with smaller roles like Algeria and the Sudan.

At the core of this pacifist's nightmare is the war against Israel. All the usual reasons impelling nations to buy arms—the acquisition of prestige among the neighbors, the calming of fear, the placating of restless populations, the purchase of the loyalty (temporary) of dangerous, coup-prone generals, the staking out of spheres of influence—are present in abundance in the Arab East, but none of these factors and no combination of any of them can explain the outpouring of wealth on weaponry. The policy of piling gun upon gun and weapons system upon weapons system is so unrestrained, so out-of-balance with the needs of nation-hood that only the gut desire to eliminate Israel can explain it in full; it is all so expensive that only this intense desire can justify it to the people.

Except for Israel, Egypt has only two neighbors, Libya and the Sudan. Neither has an industrial base or skilled manpower. Neither is in any way a physical threat; Egypt's army is twenty times bigger than Libya's and twenty-one times bigger than the Sudan's. The factors of geography (distance, deserts, logistics), psychology and intra-Arab politics make war—beyond wars of words and/or subver-sion, always permissible in the Arab ethic—between Egypt and either of its Arab neighbors virtually inconceivable.

Libya has no natural enemies, no unmet strategic needs. The superpowers guarantee its use of the Mediterranean as a highway for shipping oil. Libya's mercurial leader lends out light arms as well as heavy funds to subvert his neigh-bors, but Libya has neither reason nor capacity to grab pieces of adjoining desert, and the Arab world would hard-ly permit that anyway. Libya has a minuscule army of thirty thousand men.

Iraq is flanked on the east by Iran and on the north by Turkey. Each has three times as many people, vastly more land, much greater resources. Neither wants Iraq nor could digest it. Iraq would not dream of engaging either in major conflict. A full-scale Iraqi war with Syria or Jordan to the west seems beyond the realm even of Arab possibility. Iraq covets Kuwait but knows that Saudi Arabia would never allow a takeover. Iraq's strategic problems have eased dra-matically in recent years—its old feud with Iran is patched up and probably over for years to come, and it has succeed-ed in brutally suppressing the Kurdish rebellion, eliminat-ing the Kurdish minority as a problem and, perhaps, as a people.

And yet, among them, Egypt, Iraq and Libya have some

5,000 tanks, some 950 combat aircraft, hundreds of armored personnel carriers, many hundreds of heavy artillery pieces, scores of missiles of various kinds. All are deeply involved in the arms-purchase game.

In this deadly pastime the deck is stacked for the Arabs:

The world competes to sell to the Arabs. The U.S. is virtually Israel's only supplier. Europe would rather have ready access to Arab oil and Arab markets, and the Arabs have freely used pressure tactics and blackmail to make Europeans see that point with sufficient vividness. France turned its back on Israel early on, when the end of the Algerian war made it possible to drop a no longer convenient alliance with Israel. It took the British longer to learn that the Arabs were by far the better customers, but they did learn.

Some Arab countries manage the neat trick of buying from both East and West. Moscow and the Arabs make sure that no Eastern Bloc country will sell to Israel.

Because of this the Arabs have exclusivity on certain types of weapons and can match the Israelis with others. In the last war, Israelis in Mirages fought Arabs in the same model Mirage, thanks to Paris and Tripoli. In the next war, thanks to Washington, Israeli Skyhawks will probably fight Arab Skyhawks, Israeli M-60 tanks will duel with Arab M-60 tanks, Israelis and Arabs will fire TOW and Hawk missiles at each other.

The Arabs have so many sources that it is easy for them to move higher and higher on the scale of weapons sophistication. The Israelis must plead and argue with the U.S. for each counterbalancing weapon.

The Arabs have so many nations eager to please them that they are almost immune to pressure. When Anwar el-Sadat of Egypt was having problems early in 1975 with Soviet supplies, he went to Paris and signed a fat arms deal;

the flow in the Russian pipeline promptly began again. When Russian supplies dried up a year later, Sadat found new suppliers in Europe. Israel, dependent on the U.S., is also subject to heavy U.S. pressure; when Dr. Kissinger wanted Israel to sign a disengagement accord with Egypt without a Cairo pledge of non-belligerency or even any specific evidence of non-belligerency, he ordered a halt in the flow of certain weapons. It helped beautifully to make the point the good doctor wanted to make.

(The competition to sell to the Arabs was so great that massive sums were used to grease palms and affect sales. The Europeans, cynically wise, were seldom indiscreet enough to talk openly about such *baksheesh*: the Americans, as ever, were torn between business profit and morality. Documents pried out of the Pentagon showed that in 1973–75 five Middle Eastern agents of American firms were paid at least $18.7 million to secure military sales, ranging from missile systems for Kuwait to vehicles for Jordan. The Northrup Corp. acknowledged that it had paid middleman Adnan Khashoggi, who knew everyone worth knowing in Saudi Arabi, $450,000 for the purpose of bribing two Saudi generals to influence decisions on arms contracts. Khashoggi, admired by some as a prime example of a bold new breed of Arab money men, later developed his problems; at one point, according to an Assistant U.S. Attorney, he fled the U.S. in his private Boeing 727 "apparently" to avoid testifying about some payoff matters.)

To the world the Arabs say all the weapons they have obtained are purely defensive in nature. Among themselves, they are more blunt. The talk in Arab capitals is of another round of war eventually. The Iraqi regime's official newspaper was not impressed by the second Israeli-Egyptian disengagement accord. "The road is still open," the paper said in the government's name, "for . . . the political and military struggle to recover the usurped Arab right.'' On the second anniversary of the October, 1973, War, Syria's dominant Ba'ath party issued a long, official statement talking of ''the strategic prerequisites of the coming inevitable battle with the enemy'' and saying that the people (with a capital P) ''are always capable of making a new October.''

In the midst of shuttle diplomacy Radio Cairo told the Israelis in a Hebrew broadcast that their state ''is an illegal entity which resembles a foreign body that has not been accepted by the body''—the implication being that the body would sooner or later vomit up the foreign intruder. Weeks after the second stage Israeli-Egyptian disengagement accord, Libya's President Qaddafi was interviewed by an Arab journalist:

''*Q*. We desire and pray for the Palestinians' return home. But, if this does not happen?''

''*A*. If they cannot return home by peaceful means, they will return home by force.''

There is more, much more, to be found in the pages of Arab newspapers and transcripts of Arab radio and TV broadcasts. Saudi Arabia is America's closest friend in the Arab East. Late in 1975, the Saudi heir apparent and Deputy Premier told a Beirut newspaper that ''we support those Arab countries whose territories Israel occupies *in whatever measures they consider necessary* to regain those territories, providing they do not overlook the main issue, the Palestinian question.'' (Italics added.) Jordan is another American ally. As Dr. Kissinger was nearing the climax of the negotiations for the second Egyptian-Israeli accord, Jordan's Information Minister, Salah abu Zayd, was interviewed by a Kuwaiti newspaper. Freely acknowledging that Jordanian forces had participated in the 1973 War alongside the Syrians, abu Zayd said that Jordan ''is now preparing for the inevitable new round.'' Egypt was America's new friend. Eighteen days after the second accord was signed, the Egyptian Minister of War addressed a graduation ceremony at the Egyptian army staff college. The agreement was purely a military agreement, signed by military men, General Abdel Ghani al-Jamasi said, adding that "the state's strategic and political aim remains unchanged. It was and continues to be the liberation of the Arab territories and the restoration of the Palestinian people's rights. . . . The armed forces will not rest. Preparations continue. . . . The armed forces will act according to the spirit of October Sixth." His statement was distributed in Arabic by the Middle East News Agency and was intended for the Arab media.

None of these potential belligerents possesses arms industries of any import. They are dependent on the indulgence of greater powers. Arms are big business and the main suppliers to the Middle East are not insensible to that fact. The Soviet Union sells vast supplies of armaments to the Arabs and gives easy payment terms to the right people. In a single year—1974—the French peddled $1 billion worth of arms to the Arabian gulf states. The British, the Italians and other Europeans vie with one another for the contracts bigger powers do not preempt. The United States has become the world's most active pusher of arms to the Middle East, creating in buyers both an insatiable lust for more and an overriding need for spare parts and munitions and, in some cases, expert technicians to go with them. It is the only arms producer on the list which dares to deal with Israel. The Arabs, greedy for American arms, dare not bring their boycott to bear against American suppliers. It was therefore purely American initiative that gave the Arabs one of their most important victories over Israel—the "balancing" of arms supplies to the Middle East on a pro-rated basis. This, in diplomatic terms, is "even-handedness," the blind portioning of favor to all parties which declines to take into account the fact that there are twenty Arab nations massed against one country, Israel. It is based, instead, on a highly volatile foreign policy designed to counter Soviet influence in the Middle East by appeasing the Arabs.

It was the Soviet Union which began the dangerous escalation that has brought the area to the edge of becoming the focal point of World War III. Russia introduced the Scud, the Frog, the Kelt, all killer missiles designed for total war. It introduced heat-guided, mobile, anti-tank weapons and portable, anti-aircraft missiles. It provided the armaments which made the 1973 Yom Kippur attack on Israel a reality and, in the first ten days of that war, it jammed nearly eight thousand tons of new weapons into Cairo and Damascus. Since then, Russia has rebuilt the Egyptian and Syrian armies, modernized the Iraqi army, shoved the air confrontation up two notches by giving Egypt and Syria the prized MIG-23 fighter-bomber and stationing a squadron of Russian-piloted MIG-25s, a superb reconnaissance aircraft, in Syria.

Meanwhile, the United States embarked on its own, less cogent policy of crowd-pleasing. In the only direct and traceable response to the Soviet arms build-up in the region, it started to arm Iran heavily. At the same time, however, the U.S. inexplicably opened its arsenals to an extravaganza of arms buying by Saudi Arabia and an array of oil-inflated, minuscule emirates in the neighborhood. The lid was off. The cautious old policy which automatically precluded the sale of advanced weaponry to foreign countries was abandoned. The Arab countries immediately gobbled up some of the newest arms the U.S. could offer and supplemented the supply with purchases in Europe. In mid-1975, the Center for Defense Information, a respected

Washington think-tank, looked at what was happening and warned: "This will raise the level of destructiveness of future wars."

It was a statement of colossal anticlimax. By then, Abu Dhabi, an oil-soaked sandbox with a population of 49,000, had spent $320 million on French fighter-bombers with Mach 2 capability, while Qatar, which has twice as many people, was dickering for F-5E supersonic jets and surface-to-air missiles. Tiny Kuwait had purchased Skyhawk fighter-bombers, improved Hawk missiles, patrol boats and more. It might be considered ironic that Kuwait's Skyhawks reportedly come equipped with sophisticated defensive, weapons-delivery and navigational devices perfected by the Israelis in costly combat.

In the American view, the little oil states have their strategic eyes glued on the Gulf and are not involved in the war with Israel a thousand miles away. American policy-makers probably should monitor the Arab media more closely. In a matter of weeks the Kuwaiti Foreign Minister told one Arab newsman that Israel was created "on the torn bodies of the Arabs" and another that "from the first, Israel was set up on the basis of aggression."

Saudi Arabia is a favorite American arms customer. The 1974 package of Saudi-American agreements creating a special relationship included a security cooperation accord. The Pentagon helped shape the Saudi arms-buying spree and, according to an unpublicized report, aimed at creating a "first-rate, land combat force" and a "balanced, modern, force structure." The Saudis bought missile boats and destroyers, armored personnel carriers and M-60 tanks, jet fighters, helicopters, light tanks, surface-to-air missiles. They bought in quantity, in round numbers, hundreds of this item, hundreds of that. They signed arms contract after arms contract—$756 million for American jets, $860 million for French tanks, armored cars and a missile network. They bought quality goods, such as the maneuverable, battle-seasoned AMX light tank, used so well by the Israelis in earlier wars. They spent a tidy $1.4 billion for a complete Hawk missile system.

Eager, the United States sold the Saudis a thousand Maverick television-guided, air-to-ground missiles to go with Riyadh's new American-made F-5E Tiger jets. The Maverick is principally an anti-armor weapon and the vast, empty and hostile distances of the Saudi theatre of operations argue for the use of airborne troops rather than tanks. The Maverick would, however, be of considerable value in the quite different terrain of the Arab-Israel theatre. But when troubled congressional foreign affairs committees tried to block the sale of yet another 650 Mavericks to the Saudis as sheer overkill, the Ford Administration mobilized all its power to defeat the critics. Somehow, the Secretary of State was able to argue successfully that the Saudis were an element of stability and moderation in the Middle East.

With weapons, inevitably, there comes a variety of infrastructure. The Saudis made plans to spend no less than $16 billion on construction for the armed forces by the mid-1980s. Saudi Arabia's good friend, the U.S. Army Corps of Engineers, would supervise. And so massive was the Saudi buildup that, for the first time in American history, a private U.S. firm was authorized to find war veterans to train a foreign army. The Saudis paid out an extra $77 million to the Vinnell Corp. of California for the recruitment of a thousand former American soldiers to teach tactics, modern mechanized infantry procedures and weapons techniques to five battalions welded out of the Saudi National Guard.

The U.S. apparently saw the National Guard as a force directed toward internal security. However, the outfit's head man, Amir Abdullah ibn 'Abd Aziz Al Saud, a half-brother of the king and a Deputy Premier, was deeply concerned about "the Zionist enemy in Palestine." As quoted by the domestic service of Riyadh radio, he asked: "How can an Arab or Moslem accept the continuation of this bitter state of affairs, particularly since Zionist ambitions know no limits? These ambitions are a danger threatening the Arab and Islamic worlds and, indeed, the whole world." He also signalled that he did not see his force as inward-looking. He told Riyadh radio of his hopes for "the latest weapons." The Emir's National Guard reportedly had ordered large numbers of American-made, Cadillac-Gage, armored cars, some armed with 90-mm cannon, thereby assuring a handy degree of mobility and striking power.

The decision to train the National Guard, which one day could turn up on the battlefront against Israel, was a straightforward departure from U.S. policy. But there was no detectable policy at all in the events that led up to the horrid arms mess in the Persian Gulf. The most obvious mover and shaker, the National Security Council, had no clear hand in the decision to sell such enormous quantities of arms to the Arabs. The NSC, an agency of the executive branch, usually studies all crucial issues affecting security, but there had never been studies of the long-term impact of the Gulf arms race, nor recommendations to the U.S. government on such a matter. A *Washington Post* reporter probed Henry Kissinger's aides as the arms extravaganza developed and discovered that they judged the arms sales as "basically tactical, immediate foreign policy tools." This led to speculation that it was Kissinger himself, once head of the NSC, who had pushed the weapons sales. "He probably preferred the flexibility that comes with these tactical decisions," one of the great man's aides reportedly

211

said, "rather than holding to a hard policy that could have come out of a study."

The "foreign policy" arguments most often advanced in explaining the arming of Iran and the Arabs—by which most people mean, in this context, Saudi Arabia—are fourfold:

It was a military deterrent for the Soviet Union.

It would ensure internal stability for both countries.

It would solidify ties with the United States.

It would spur the Arabs to make peace with Israel.

The facts are these:

Anytime the Soviet Union wants to, it can roll right over both Iran and Saudi Arabia, to say nothing of Abu Dhabi.

Neither Phantom jets nor SAM missiles could help either the Saudis or the Iranians in the sort of bloody rebellion their repressive regimes invite. In the words of the Center for Defense Information: "Political and social change is inevitable in the Persian Gulf and U.S. programs that create excessive military establishments actually stimulate political upheaval."

Ties with the U.S. are as solid as they are going to get. The Gulf countries are compulsive biters of the hand that feeds them, munitions or no munitions.

The Arabs are going to use those arms against Israel.

This last point has already been foreshadowed by an exchange between a New Jersey Senator and the U.S. Department of State. In mid-1975, Senator Clifford Case asked for reaction on some disturbing reports about the use to which American arms were being put. Case, a Republican, had heard that F-5E jet fighters sold to Saudi Arabia had participated in a military exercise in Syria. Furthermore, there were rumors that senior Egyptian air force officers had flown in Phantom fighter-bombers sold to Iran.

Confirmation of both reports came from Robert J. McCloskey, Assistant Secretary of State for Congressional Affairs. He added a comment which had earlier been voiced by critics of the Gulf arms race: "There is no way we can provide absolute assurance that there would not be unauthorized transfers of military equipment between one Arab country and another, particularly in a period of stress."

Alfred L. Atherton, Assistant Secretary of State for Near Eastern Affairs, had a more cheerful interpretation of the situation. Although he reluctantly conceded that American arms could be used by Saudi Arabia against Israel, he assured a group of Congressmen that Saudi weapons "will not significantly affect the balance of forces."

Atherton confirmed that the Saudis maintained one brigade in Jordan on Israel's eastern frontier and a second in Syria on Israel's northeastern flank. No mention was made of Tabuq in the northwestern corner of Saudi Arabia itself. Tabuq is far from Riyadh and the climate is awful, but Tabuq has one advantage: it is 130 miles from the southern tip of Israel and the strategic Israeli harbor of Elath, entry port for Persian oil. The Saudis are expanding their air base at Tabuq, at a reported cost of more than $1 billion, with the help of the U.S. Army Corps of Engineers.

Tabuq alone would not answer the problem. A Saudi air force joining a new war against Israel would have to depend in large measure on the overburdened and not notably efficient airdromes of Egypt, Syria and Jordan. But tanker planes for air-to-air refueling would enable the Saudis to strike out from home without difficulty. And sure enough, late in the summer of 1976, the Saudis were reported buying twenty huge American transport planes for conversion into tankers.

One of the most ingenuous misconceptions about the Yom Kippur attack on Israel is that Syria and Egypt fought the war. The truth is that the Yom Kippur War was a concerted attack upon Israel from Egyptian and Syrian territory by Egypt, Syria and the following countries:

Jordan, which chose the better part of valor and declined to attack directly from its own borders with Israel. Instead, King Hussein sent two armored brigades to Syria; nearly one hundred Jordanian tanks, supported by three artillery batteries, attacked Israeli positions at the height of the Golan fighting and about half the tanks were lost.

Algeria, which sent two squadrons of fighter planes, one squadron of Soviet Ilyushin-28 bombers, one hundred fifty tanks and an armored brigade to Egypt. All saw action.

Morocco, which supplied 2,500 troops to the Syrians. Trained by American officers, they reportedly were transferred to Syria on Soviet naval vessels. They saw action.

Iraq, a fully engaged combatant, with two armored divisions, an infantry division and aircraft in Syria. The Iraqi Third Armored Division, with twenty thousand men and 320 tanks, was committed to the battle in the central Golan and suffered heavy losses. Iraqi MIGs went into action over the Golan on the third day of the war. (Their Syrian hosts reportedly shot down twenty Iraqi MIGs with poorly aimed SAM missiles.)

Sudan, which sent 4,500 men to Egypt.

Kuwait, which had stationed a few units on the Suez since 1969 and, it seems, finally committed them.

Lebanon, which seconded its radar to the Syrians, provided Syria with electric power and permitted its resident terrorists to shell Israeli villages from one end of their common border to the other.

Tunisia, with a battalion in the Nile Valley.

Saudi Arabia, which put a brigade into Syria and, ignoring American conditions of sale, sent a squadron of U.S.-made Bell 205 Iroquois helicopters to Egypt.

214

Libya, which had a brigade in Egypt.

In the words of Anwar el-Sadat: "Saudi Arabia, Kuwait, Abu Dhabi and all our brothers helped." Interestingly, the war against Israel made brothers of the most radical and the most conservative of Arab states and caused feuds to be temporarily forgotten.

The brothers helped in another, little-publicized manner, too. While the world focused on Egypt and Syria, the so-called "non-confrontation states" were busily keeping confronters in supplies. Sadat, in a graceful speech of acknowledgment broadcast on Cairo radio, described this "Arab solidarity" as "one of the most magnificent achievements of the October war."

"There is Algeria," he said. "President Boumédiene, without contacting anybody, left secretly during the battle for the Soviet Union and paid $100 million for Egypt and $100 million for Syria. He asked the Soviet Union to send the arms requested by Egypt and Syria quickly.

"Now I deal with Saudi Arabia. . . . Before the battle, Feisal purchased helicopters for Egypt and gave them as gifts. . . . He did not stop at this. He purchased Mirage aircraft for Egypt. . . .

"Our brothers in Kuwait adopted the same stand. . . . They also bought us some planes and asked us if we required anything else, as for example, oil, arms and so forth. . . ."

The Saudi gift list grew after the war to include thirty-eight French Mirage 3's, as well as British Lightning interceptor jets and dozens of light tanks. As for the oil kingdom's own ballooning military machine, Saudi Crown Prince Fahd, the effective head of the government, said in 1976 that it was to be "a force in the defense of the Arab nation and the Arab cause." The term "Arab nation" is meant to include all Arabs, not just Saudis; the "Arab cause'' is usually interpreted to mean the crusade against Israel.

The Kuwaitis were also open-handed to a fault after the 1973 war. They kindly ordered twenty Mirage F-1s—France's very best and a very costly item—for Egypt. Both the Saudis and the Kuwaitis were also ready to treat the Jordanians to some fine weapons for eventual use on the Israeli frontier. Hussein was, in fact, the happy recipient of some very lovely offers from a variety of sources. Presumably because of the moderation which kept him off the official—though not the actual—combat list in the Yom Kippur War, Hussein was allowed to buy TOW anti-tank missiles from the U.S. America went on to approve the transfer of twenty-four F-5E Tiger jets to Jordan from Iran, a Moslem if not an Arab brother, and then arranged to sell Jordan thirty-one more Tigers of a much-improved model. To this, the U.S. added the construction of a $100 million tank facility with the potential for becoming the main repair and revision center for the entire Eastern front in time of war with Israel.

Hussein, once the most stolid and loyal of America's Arab associates, also learned the standard Third World trick of flirting with both West and East in order to bargain for more and better weapons, such as a collection of surface-to-air missiles handily suitable for defense and/or for support of offensive operations west of the Jordan river. (In the end the Saudis obligingly put up $540 million so Hussein could have an American system.) The Hashemite king was on record, in an interview with a Beirut magazine, as saying that he needed the new weapons he was so eagerly collecting in order to help Syria in any new war with Israel.

Hussein, the so-called moderate, went on to institute a military draft for the first time. And he was big enough, broadminded enough, to put aside an old and bitter quarrel

216

and to form what was essentially a joint command with Syria.

For some reason Western journalists interpreted the Jordanian-Syrian command setup as defensive in nature. The Syrians and Jordanians, in talking to their own peoples, did not advertise it that way at all. Hussein visited Damascus to arrange the unprecedented command. The visit was climaxed by a joint communiqué, broadcast simultaneously on Damascus and Amman radios. "There is no substitute for military power," the communiqué read. It spoke of the "total liberation of the land," a word construction generally understood in the Arab world to mean all the land between the Mediterranean and the Jordan River. It proclaimed "the special importance of mobilizing the resources of the Arab nation and throwing these resources into the battle against the Zionist enemy."

The Western world paid little attention to the communiqué. And yet the joint statement went into organizational details and gave the "supreme command council" the right to discuss "the issues of peace and war" and to make "joint and coordinated decisions and stands regarding" those issues of war and peace. Later, Hussein demonstrated that he was serious about it all by sending 10,000 of his troops to a major joint exercise on Syrian soil.

Syria was doing beautifully on its own. The Russians swiftly replaced all of Syria's 1973 losses—more than one thousand tanks, one hundred combat aircraft, fifteen SAM batteries—and then added an array of new weapons, from T-62 battle tanks through electronic devices to unpiloted drone aircraft. Syria's air strength increased by at least 25 per cent in the first two years after the 1973 war, and Syria became the first country outside the Soviet Union to receive the advance swing-wing MIG-23. In 1973 the Syrians had not hesitated to aim ground-to-ground Frog rockets at targets in the heart of Israel; now the Soviets gave Syria the bigger, more brutal Scud missile. Ever thoughtful, the Soviets sent two thousand advisers to teach the Syrians to use the new equipment. Ironically, Syria's purchases from the Soviets were largely made possible by heavy subsidies from ultra-conservative Saudi Arabia; when war against Israel is planned, there are no radicals, no conservatives.

So laden with sophisticated arms had the Syrians become that, for the first time, military specialists deemed Syria capable of launching a major attack on Israel without a coordinated assault from Egypt. War with Israel was natural to the Syrians. Comrade Abdallah al-Ahwar, a top Syrian Ba'ath party official, told the Lebanese News Agency: "We have been in a constant state of war with the Zionist enemy since 1948. This state will continue to exist until we recover the rights of our Arab nation in full." The ever hopeful U.S. State Department saw occasional glimmers of moderation in Syria, but Syria's President al-Assad was frank. Asked by a *Newsweek* correspondent how fighting might erupt again on the northern front, al-Assad said that Israel might try to exploit the Lebanese crisis, but added: "Then there is the possibility that we might decide that the time is suitable for the resumption of fighting to liberate our land."

Syria's eastern neighbor, Iraq, also received some Scud missiles from Russia, and increased its ability to mass quickly on the Syrian or Jordanian frontier with Israel when Moscow provided Baghdad with large numbers of tank transporters. Emboldened by oil wealth, Iraq looked beyond the Soviets for arms for the first time in a decade and a half; France, ignoring Baghdad radio's constant flood of hate of Israel, sold Iraq $70 million worth of combat helicopters. But Moscow kept Baghdad happy with high-flying MIG-23s and TU-22 supersonic bombers, and there were reports that the Russians had been obliging enough to provide planes and pilots for strikes against the Kurdish rebels.

There is on record a major arms transfer in which a "non-confrontation state" blatantly violated its pledge to keep its purchases at home. As the French can testify, Libya's Qaddafi, a man as good as his word, sneaked some forty Mirage 3's to Egypt right after the Yom Kippur War began. The Israelis, who had to fight them off, immediately told the world about it, but the French chose to ignore this embarrassing bit of intelligence because they were then playing the innocent game of Embargo to All Parties, which amounted to an anti-Israel exercise. When they got around to lifting the embargo, the French sold Libya fifty Mirage 5's and forty F-1's.

The Libyans are a munition salesman's effulgent dream. They can't even fly all the planes they buy. They keep some of them in storage and lend others out. With no declared enemies but Israel, and an army of 35,000, Libya is stockpiling arms for something which looks suspiciously like the apocalypse. Libya's chief suppliers besides the French are the Soviets, and hardware on hand or on order includes 1,100 tanks, 800 armored personnel carriers, 29 MIG-23's, 50 SAM batteries, 12 Super Frelon helicopters and 12 French missile boats and, most ominous of all, a number of long-range Scud missiles. Awed estimates of the sum he has committed to pay the Soviets for weapons range up to $8 billion; Libya's arms budget for 1975–76 alone was more than $2 billion. The likeliest beneficiary of his over-stocked warehouse in the next war with Israel is Egypt, his next-door neighbor to the east, which has the men to run Libya's machines and which showed itself magnanimous enough in 1973 to put aside old differences with Qaddafi and accept his generous loan of those Mirage 3's. In case of real need, a new Egyptian-Libyan feud could be put aside via one telephone call and Libya's big T-62 tanks could reach the Egyptian front in twenty-four to thirty-six hours.

In general, the Arabs disguise their plans behind soft

219

talk. Not Qaddafi of Libya. He has been frank to the point of brutality. In mid-1975 he honored a *Los Angeles Times* correspondent with an interview. "Israelis," he told the seasoned reporter, "can leave and go back to their countries which they came from and leave Palestine for the Palestinians." The alternative, he said, will be a war in which "unified Arab armies" will overwhelm Israel. He himself, Qaddafi added, was preparing for such a holy war. Qaddafi indicated, the American reporter noted carefully, "that his substantial purchase of weapons . . . is not so much for Libya's defense, but is a reserve for the future all-out Arab attack on Israel which he envisions." A few days after a new arms deal with Moscow, Qaddafi told Arab listeners he would fight "until the Zionist state is destroyed." Some people laugh at Libyan pretensions, but it *has* the weapons—and the money to buy more. Much of that money, ironically, comes from the United States—in 1976 Libya was selling oil to the U.S. at the rate of $1.5 billion a year.

As for Sadat, he wants more—and more. The dramatic Soviet air- and sea-lift in October, 1973, promptly replaced most of Egypt's war losses. Moscow dutifully supplied hundreds of tanks and 100 fighter aircraft, replaced dozens of missile batteries and hundreds of wrecked armored cars and artillery pieces. Then relations grew complex. The Soviets had learned something Washington was later to ignore—that Cairo was unreliable. And, having rescued Egypt during the war, Moscow naturally wanted some tidbits of political repayment and at least partial repayment of the billions Cairo owed on earlier arms shipments. The flow of weapons slowed, then stopped, then was renewed again, then slowed again. Despite all the publicity attached to the slowdown, however, Sadat was able to grow in strength. His air force received twenty-five MIG-23's, an innovation, and a number of Sukhoi 7's with all the required spare parts and ammunition. The number of deadly Scud missile launchers in Egyptian hands went up from 9 to at least 24, the number of launchers for Luna short-range, ground-to-ground missiles from 12 to 18.

Gratitude is not an Arab virtue. In 1976, in an act which seized the headlines and pleased the State Department, Sadat ceremoniously abrogated the 15-year treaty of "unbreakable friendship" signed four years earlier with the Soviet Union, considered at that time "a true and sincere friend who supported us in our darkest hour." Jaundiced Western specialists, remembering that the Egyptian "expulsion" of the Soviet experts in 1972 was followed by new arms deals with Moscow leading directly to the Yom Kippur War, doubted the depth of the new "split." Western statesmen, from Washington to Bonn, were eager to believe Sadat because it was convenient to do so.

The fact was that Sadat, growing more sophisticated, had already set out to develop new sources of arms supply. His intent, said the well-informed in Cairo, was not only to acquire more weaponry but to end dependence on one supplier; a single supplier, Sadat had found, could inhibit the exercise of power. And, with the help of the West, Sadat could look forward to solving his re-equipment problems in a couple of years.

For all his cries of poverty, he found hundreds of millions of dollars for new weapons; he maintained a standing army of no less than 325,000 men, including two armored divisions and six brigades of special forces; he had 2,200 heavy guns against Israel's 660-plus and many of his 2,600 armored full-track personnel carriers, all Soviet-made, were almost brand new. In fact, although his people were impoverished, his development needs urgent, his debts crushing, he could spend an estimated one-fourth of his Gross National Product on defense. Courtesy of cash from

221

the oil Arabs, he bought dozens of Mirage 5's, thirty combat helicopters from the British, electronics from the Italians. He worked out plans to modernize aging Soviet tanks with Western 105-mm guns and Western engines. The experts quarreled as to whether he had ordered or was merely considering purchase of impressive numbers of the British-French Jaguar strike aircraft and more F-1's. He went shopping for additional arms across Western Europe, and the new Arab Defense Procurement Organization—made up of Saudi Arabia, Kuwait and the United Arab Emirates—dutifully conferred with British and French bankers about financing. The oil Arabs put aside a tidy $1 billion to set up a pan-Arab arms industry in Egypt—designed, in part, to balance the advantage a home-grown weapons industry gave the Israelis—and were ready to invest an additional $1 billion a year for three years in the name of Arab self-sufficiency. Sadat received offers of help in implementing the project from British and French manufacturers and the benevolent French government; the idea was to start with production of light strike aircraft and helicopters. Ever pragmatic, never one to let past loyalties get in the way, Sadat also carried out a neat diplomatic exercise and got the People's Republic of China to donate engines and spare parts for his MIG-17's and -21's. The lovely new friendship for peace was cemented with the signing in Peking of a military protocol and the promise of more supplies. Sadat remained a master juggler of the powers. Months after his noisy renunciation of the Soviet friendship treaty, Egypt was still quietly receiving military spare parts from the USSR. On the third anniversary of the Yom Kippur attack, Sadat could celebrate the occasion by displaying surface-to-surface Scuds, British-made anti-tank missiles, French-British Gazelle helicopters and Soviet MIG-23 interceptors.

222

Although he preached peace, Sadat could not refrain from gloating—in Arabic, to Arabs—about how he tricked the world in October, 1973. In his reminiscences on Cairo radio about his game-playing with the Russian experts in 1972, he said that "not even the most brilliant political analysts in the West were able to understand it. They all thought I would not go to war." The possibility that he might strike again was repeatedly hinted at in Cairo's Arabic media. The Chairman of the Board of a leading Cairo daily wrote that the second Sinai accord "must not be misunderstood. It is a military agreement. Also, it is temporary. . . . The day the Arab territories are liberated from Zionist occupation and the Palestinians regain their legitimate rights to their land, all these agreements will become history." Western specialists believed that, for all his hand-wringing, Sadat fighting alone could defend himself well in the Sinai even before absorbing all the new weaponry and, with other Arab armies fighting alongside, could effectively attack Israel.

Given all this, Sadat's requests from the United States were low key—temporarily, that is. All he wanted was defensive weaponry. He had his own definition of defensive weaponry. It encompassed TOW anti-tank missiles and F-5E fighters. TOWs, mounted on jeeps and armored cars, can join tanks, infantry or a combination of the two in offensive strikes. F-5E's usually come equipped with Sidewinder air-to-air missiles and have range enough to patrol deep into the Sinai.

Sadat settled for six C-130 transports (since it was an election year, he knew that the Administration had to move cautiously), but that was a precedent and, clearly, he would be back for more. On the whole, he said, he would be content with 40 per cent of the total which Israel receives in weaponry from the U.S. each year. His sources are numerous, while Israel is dependent on the U.S., which puts Egypt's request into the category of quintessential gall.

Israel's strategic planners have argued for years that, although Israel lacks the resources to maintain a one-to-one balance of arms with the Arabs, Israel's very survival depends on maintenance of an overall one-to-three ratio of military power. Such a rough ratio would take into account the relative values of various weapons and different branches of the military and weigh in Israel's internal lines of communications, superior command structure and fighting ability, superior economic and administrative infrastructure. The Pentagon and the CIA generally have accepted this reasoning.

There is, of course, a physical limit to the values of such imponderables as fighting ability, command brilliance and morale in overcoming sheer numbers. There were, therefore, distress signals in the ratios listed by a senior Israeli defense official as quoted by Drew Middleton, the veteran Military Affairs Correspondent of *The New York Times*: In missiles, the Arabs had a twelve-to-one superiority; in tanks and aircraft, three-to-one; in artillery, five-to-one. It was obvious that those ratios could, and almost certainly would, shift further toward imbalance as the arms race grew more and more insane.

The imbalance was impressive enough even when confined to Israel vs. the most immediate threats posed by its neighbors—Egypt, Syria, Jordan and Iraq. The International Institute of Strategic Studies, whose calculations are universally accepted as the geo-military word from Sinai, added up these contrasting totals as of mid-1975:

Army strength, 620,000 for the four Arab states as against 135,000 for Israel. (Full mobilization of reserves would bring the Israeli total to 375,000 but would increase Arab strength as well.)

Medium tanks, 5,840 for the Arab states as opposed to 2,700 for Israel.

Field artillery, 3,330 for the four Arab powers as against 1,500 for Israel.

Submarines, 12 for the Arabs and 2 for Israel.

Missile boats, 27 for the Arab powers and 15 for Israel.

Tactical aircraft, 1,201 for the four Arab states as against 481 for Israel.

The figures offer cold proof of the intensity of the Middle East arms race. Compare the above with, for example, these IISS figures covering some of Europe's industrial powers: Britain has 345,000 men in her armed forces, France has 461 combat aircraft, Italy has 1,300 medium tanks.

A study reportedly prepared by the Pentagon for its own use, and quoted by columnist Jack Anderson, presented an even more sobering account of the fire power of Egypt, Syria, Jordan, Iraq, Libya and Saudi Arabia:

The six Arab countries had 4 times as many combat aircraft as the Israelis; 19 times as many anti-aircraft missiles; 3 times as many combat ships and submarines.

The six Arab countries had more than 1,500 jet fighters, supersonic and subsonic. The Israelis had a total of 426 combat aircraft, of which 206 are supersonic. Egypt had 347 supersonic fighters and the Syrians had 338. The two countries between them had 62 MIG-23's, a plane which outperforms the Phantom, the best Israel had.

The Arabs had 2,530 pilots, 1,740 of them trained to fly jets. They had a total of 78,600 airmen. Israel had 1,100 pilots, 700 of them qualified for jets, and 19,000 airmen.

The six Arab states had 15,285 SAM missiles of various types. Israel had 800 anti-aircraft missiles, including the short-range Chaparral. The Arabs had 2,678 missile launchers, of which 399 are in the field. The Israelis had 114 launchers, 15 of them on the front. During the Yom Kippur War, the report reminded us, the Arabs shot down one Israeli plane in combat. The remainder of Israel's losses, 120 aircraft, were destroyed by SAM's.

Israel had a navy of 5,000 seamen. The Arabs had five times that number. Israel had 18 missile boats and one submarine. The Arabs had 49 destroyers, submarines and missile boats.

The Pentagon's conclusions? Israel would win the next war but the victory would be "costly." How costly? The CIA, which is very good at that sort of thing, has figured it at 8,000 Israeli dead and a minimum of 36,000 wounded, or more than 3 times the death toll and 6 times the total number of wounded in the Yom Kippur War.

Israel has 3 million people. In terms of the population of the United States, those casualty rates would be proportionately equivalent to 528,000 dead and at least 2,400,000 wounded.

13

The Fifth Round

The word the Arabs use when they speak of peace with Israel, even in rejection, is *salaam*; it is a word that has no exact English equivalent. It is often confused with *shalom*, a Hebrew word meaning, quite simply, peace, normal conduct between men and nations. *Salaam* is an equivocal term which does not extend to reconciliation. There is another word for that: *sulh*. Only *sulh* is binding on all parties, and in Arab tribal society it is a solemn undertaking which becomes effective only with the completion of a *sulha*, a peace-making ceremony at which former enemies exchange gifts and share bread and meat.

A translation often used for *salaam* is non-belligerency. Here is Anwar el-Sadat confronted by an American TV reporter who wanted to know more about the Arab vision of peace: "This we must leave to the next generation to decide. I think if we can achieve the end to the state of belligerency officially, let us leave to that generation to decide what will come after."

Sadat was a bit more specific in an interview with a correspondent for *Le Monde*: While "ready to conclude a peace agreement with Israel . . . I think that it is still too soon to speak of diplomatic relations or open frontiers. . . . I leave to the next generation the trouble of deciding if it is possible not only to coexist with the Jewish state but also to cooperate with it. Everything depends, moreover, on the behavior of Israel after the establishment of peace."

Sadat was using language as it is used in Orwell's *1984*. Black is white; truth is falsehood; peace is war. Sadat's "peace agreement," his "establishment of peace," offered as a concession of historic importance, was simply a formal cease-fire. (Even this "peace," Sadat told an American editor, could be discussed only *after* Israel retreated from the Golan Heights, the Sinai and the West Bank, an act which would deprive Israel of all strategic depth *before* "peace.") There would be no trade, no diplomatic relations, no recognition, no tourism, no human contact whatsoever, no links by telephone, airliner, ship, mail, cablegram, telex. Israel would remain a pariah. There would be no movement or link which might lead in time to understanding, or a reduction in tension, or a diminution of the danger of war. There would be nothing which might prompt that "next generation" to make the bold experiment and sample peace. Libya's Qaddafi, as usual, was most direct and honest in his description: "It is not peace as peace, as we all know what it means. It is armistice."

Both Arabs and Israelis understand the symbolic significance of these words—peace, cease-fire, *salaam, sulh*. The second-stage Egyptian-Israeli disengagement accord was held up for many weeks mainly because Egypt would not agree to a pledge of "non-belligerency"—*that* would have granted the enemy a coveted status of legitimacy—and in the end, Israel had to accept a much vaguer and less satisfactory formulation. The only direct Israeli-Arab talks *ever* held were those between an Egyptian General and his Israeli counterpart at km. 101 on the Cairo-Suez road just after the Yom Kippur War. The generals were professional military men and as such got along fairly well. During one break in the complex talks, they walked together in the desert and, as soldiers—even generals—will, they talked of peace. The Israeli General, according to Matti Golan in his *Secret Conversations of Henry Kissinger*, asked whether the Egyptian meant *salaam* or *sulh*. The Egyptian smiled and said, *salaam*; *sulh* would require many years to develop.

Most people regard "armistice" as a step toward peace. It need not be. There are other distinct possibilities. An armistice can continue indefinitely (e.g., the cease-fire arrangement on the 38th parallel in Korea) with no substantive contact between the signatories. An armistice can signify an absence of classical warfare but a continuation of war by other means, politics, diplomatic, economic, paramilitary. An armistice can deteriorate into war and it can be used to prepare for war. In the Arab-Israel conflict, only the first of these possibilities—the step toward peace—has never been tried.

Over the past three decades, there have been long periods of armistice in the Middle East. The Arabs, always after defeat in the field, always reluctantly, have signed agreements which recognized cease-fire lines, pledged demilitarization in certain areas or accepted the presence of UN observers in this place or that. These were purely temporary arrangements in Arab eyes, useful as periods of convalescence between wars. The series of armistice agreements in 1949, which earned UN mediator Ralph Bunche the Nobel Prize for peace, were "complete and enduring"; they were to be superseded by peace agreements; their purpose, as one of the agreements put it, was "to facilitate the transition from the present truce to permanent peace." And when the arduous negotiations were completed and all the papers signed, Bunche said without reservation: "The military phase of the Palestine conflict is ended."

However, the cease-fire agreements of 1949 were followed by economic war and *fedayeen* raids and were used as justification for the Suez blockade on Israeli shipping and cargoes. The cease-fire following the 1956 flare-up was used as a cloak for preparations for 1967. The cease-fire following the 1967 war provided time to prepare for the 1973 attack. There is no reason—beyond Sadat's fuzzy words about the next generation—to believe that the pattern was broken by the three accords of 1974 and 1975. Each was called a "disengagement agreement" rather than an armistice or cease-fire. This was purely a semantic matter; Dr. Kissinger thought disengagement sounded better.

The Arabs themselves saw no significance in disengagement. They did not believe that the 1973 war, glorious though it had been, had achieved the Arab goal. In the midst of shuttle diplomacy, Hafez al-Assad of Syria said: "As far as we are concerned, the war is not over. It will not be over . . . unless the Palestinian people's rights are restored in full." He underlined the point in a later speech: ". . . Israel is occupying all of Palestine and . . . displacing its people. . . . All international charters . . . give the right to a people whose land is occupied to use all means at their disposal to liberate their land." Mohammed Hassenein Heikal, the Egyptian journalist, said: "The importance of the October War can be appreciated when it is viewed as a bridge to the next war. It was not the last war."

The Arabs take a long view of history. They are in no hurry. The war that has already lasted thirty years will take as long as necessary. As Egypt's Arab Socialist Union has pointed out, it is a struggle for generations. Yasir Arafat, after praising the decision to attack on Yom Kippur 1973 as "an important turning point," said: "Perhaps in ten years' time another decision will be taken to liquidate the arrogant enemy entirely."

There are two major obstacles in the way of implementing such a decision. The first is Israel's military skill, strength and devotion coupled with Israel's economic and human infra-structure. The second is that, for a complex of reasons, the United States is not at this time willing to tolerate the armed destruction of Israel.

The problem—and it is a subject of constant discussion in Arab capitals—is how to overcome these obstacles. The preferred tactic in the years just after the Yom Kippur War called for the creation of an Arab mini-state in "liberated" areas of Palestine. Such a state, in the words of Arafat's Chief Lieutenant, would be "a revolutionary base for our people." Against such a state the borders of Israel would provide little protection; there are no natural barriers along their lengths. Struggle would be in the cards. It would begin—perhaps immediately, more likely after a productive pause for preparation—with incursion, theft and raid, shelling of farms and cities, sniping. The clock would roll back to the 1950s when Egypt and Jordan sent marauders across from the West Bank and Gaza in such numbers that Israeli civilians traveled the highways in convoy with armored escort. The struggle would be accompanied by the usual political and economic attacks. Tensions would build, the economic and psychological strain on Israel would be immense.

An exact blueprint of what might then happen has apparently not been set down by Arab war planners. But the Arabs know the Israelis of old, and they would anticipate that in time Israel would reach a breaking point and lash out in hope of winning a few years of quiet. Such an Israeli move would be fine with the Arabs. For Israel, even if it won on the ground, would lose in terms of relative national strength. There are 150 million Arabs and 3 million Israelis; the Arabs have tens of oil billions, the Israelis have debts.

While he was still talking disengagement with Henry Kissinger, while he was spreading a message of peace and moderation to the West, Anwar el-Sadat spoke with frankness to students at Alexandria University: "The most important effect of the October War lies in what is done to Israel's existence and future. . . . The presence of Israel in the Arab region and the possibility of its continued existence have been fundamentally shaken. . . . A process of disintegration and self-destruction has begun to show. If the Arabs continue to be strong, it is almost certain that this will cause Israel's withering or gradual extinction." Sadat did not need to spell out the obvious: that "withering" takes various forms—a rise in emigration, a fall-off in foreign investments (which dropped by half in the year after the 1973 war), a slowdown in local investment, the incredible expenses of a bout of warfare (the Yom Kippur War cost Israel one year's Gross National Product), a ruinous inflation stimulated by the defense burden (which absorbed nearly half the government's budget in 1975). It is ironic that the West, whether consciously or not, aids and abets this strategy of erosion by accepting the Arab boycott, feeding the arms race without any semblance of logic, and adopting diplomatic positions which encourage the Arabs to believe there is no need for serious reappraisal of their posture toward Israel.

A mini-state, clearly enough, would speed along the entire "withering" process dramatically. The mini-state, ideally, would be created through the application of international pressure, particularly from the United States, so extreme that Israel would have to retreat with nothing in return and without the need for the Arabs to fire a shot. Such an achievement would give the Arab states the valuable commodity of time, time for Sadat to shore up Egypt's economy and reorganize its army, time for the Saudis to absorb their glut of arms, time for the eastern front to be solidified.

There was an obvious and possibly fatal flaw, touched upon earlier in these pages, to such a plan. The comparatively moderate Arab forces, reversing von Clausewitz, were ready to consider diplomacy as a form of warfare and perhaps to use it accordingly, at a Geneva conference or elsewhere. But the rejectionists, the fundamentalists of the Arab world, served endless notice of intent to sabotage any agreement, no matter how favorable, which settled even temporarily for less than all of Palestine.

Only foreign observers, ever hopeful, saw signs for hope in the war involving the terrorists in Lebanon. The hope was almost certainly illusory. For the war, while exceedingly complicated, was in large measure an intra-Arab struggle over power and tactics, not goals or principles. The latter remained unchanged. While many thousands died in the conflict in Lebanon, the Arab world competed within itself to prove dedication to the crusade for Palestine. The PLO, though bloodied and reduced on the ground, was crowned a full voting member of the Arab League in September, 1976, thereby theoretically achieving equal status with Egypt and Syria and eighteen other Arab states. It was an exercise designed to demonstrate that, despite Lebanon, the Palestinian cause—though not necessarily its leadership—remained unsullied, valid and worthy of political, diplomatic and financial support to the end that a twenty-first Arab state might be created.

These same foreign observers saw reason for optimism in

the fact that there were combatants in the desperate war in Lebanon who tacitly accepted Israeli assistance. That, however, seemed a matter of convenience—and reversible. Certainly, it was not without precedent. King Hussein had not minded at all when Israel massed forces in the Jordan Valley to help stall a Syrian invasion column aimed at Amman during Jordan's bloody suppression of the terrorists in 1970. Three years later Hussein rushed men, armor and artillery to Syria to participate in the Yom Kippur War—while carefully guarding his lines to his once and, he hoped, future subjects by maintaining the flow of trade with the Israel-held West Bank.

Syria was supposedly committed to a new moderation. As the Lebanese fighting raged, however, a high official in Damascus said: "Syria is the base for the Palestinian cause and the base of their strength. There is no Palestinian revolution without the Syrian army." And Hafez al-Assad, in a major policy speech, said: "Any talk about war [with Israel], any talk about the liberation of Palestine without Syria is ignorance and misleads the people." Syria's strategic ability to contribute to the liberation of Palestine increased substantially as a result of the Syrian army's advances in south-central Lebanon.

Syria's most serious complaint was not that the PLO was fighting but that it was fighting in the wrong place. Defense Minister Mustafa Tlas, the man who had enlightened the Syrian parliament about the fate of certain Israeli prisoners in the 1973 war, put it succinctly in an article in a Damascus newspaper in the autumn of 1976: "The Palestine Liberation Organization . . . has forgotten that its prime objective is to return to Palestine and not to participate in power in Lebanon."

The question, then, was not of outlawing the terrorists, but of controlling them. Assad's Syria continued to shelter the practiced killers of Saiqa, differing from other branches of the terror movement principally in that they sallied forth to kill only on orders from Damascus.

The war in Lebanon, naturally, whetted appetites and, indeed, was fed by ambitions. Assad, for example, dreamed the old dream of a Greater Syria. During the 1976 struggle, with his troops occupying more than two-thirds of Lebanon, he reminded the Arab world that "historically, Syria and Lebanon formed one country and one people." In the midst of the war, Damascus radio reported, Assad received a delegation of "Palestinian brothers" who stressed the "nationalist ties" between Syria and Palestine and, to the obvious satisfaction of Damascus, noted that "history and reality attest that Palestine is the southern part of Syria."

Just how a Greater Syria might be organized was an item for some future agenda. It might not necessarily require an omnipotent unitary state but could encompass a cantonized Lebanon, a subordinate ally in Jordan, a puppet Palestinian entity. The possibilities were various and tantalizing, but subject to challenge by Arab rivals.

Whatever the goals of the individual belligerent states, Lebanon marked a deep trauma for all the Arab world. Every other Arab earthquake in modern times has brought its after-shocks—the shame of 1948 resulted in the ouster of Egypt's King Farouk and the launching of the turbulent, expansionist Nasserite adventure; the disgrace of 1956 led to the bloody overthrow of the pro-Western Iraqi dynasty and the skyrocketing rise of Soviet influence; the disaster of 1967 brought radically new regimes to Egypt and Syria and gave a rebirth to terror. Each defeat, too, was followed by new efforts to eradicate the interloper, Israel. The excesses in Lebanon, the ruin of a nation, could not be hidden by screens of words. The tornadoes raised by Lebanon are bound to rage on and on or, artificially suppressed, to breed new storm centers. The cruel war in Lebanon can only create new shame, new self-hate—and reason to fear there would be a new lashing out to save honor, to salve pride, to demonstrate devotion to the Arab cause. Israel remains, an infuriating presence. Inevitably, there is renewed discussion of a fifth round of classic warfare once inter-Arab peace can be restored.

In that connection it is instructive to explore a study, prepared before the Lebanese explosion, entitled *Future Arab Strategy in the Light of the Fourth War.* The author is a Palestinian named al-Haytnam al-Ayubi, former lieutenant-colonel in the Syrian Army, former chief of the military arm of the Popular Front for the Liberation of Palestine, skilled military analyst, author of books on guerrilla warfare. *The Future Arab Strategy* was published by a scholarly press in Beirut and translated by the Israeli Universities' Study Group for Middle Eastern Affairs.

Al-Ayubi's vision of the next phase of the war against Israel can be compared to the chase of a swift-footed animal by a pack of wolves. It would proceed in relays, with fresh predators taking up the chase in turn until the quarry drops in exhaustion and the entire pack closes in for the kill.

The juggernaut attack the Arabs launched against Israel in 1973 cannot be repeated, al-Ayubi explains, because "threatening Israel with collapse would automatically elicit an American alert." Instead, he sees a long war carried out by the regular military forces of the massed Arab countries operating under a single unified command and "using the tactics of conventional war and the spirit of guerrilla war." The forces engaged in relays would include army brigades or divisions, air units, naval forces, submarines and missile batteries. There would be "heavy, unexpected and swift blows over a long period of time, on condition that the scope, target, depth and timing of these strikes give the appearance of being limited so that no strong American response is called for." Tactics would be adapted to geographic conditions. Thus, the Sinai would be "appropriate for armored or aerial guerrilla warfare." The attacks would be carried out from "the encircling states," but the non-confrontation states would have to give up their old proxy roles and send in trained special-operations teams.

The objective would be to "erode Israel's morale and ensure the accumulation of emotional shocks and shattering blows" to the point where Israel would be forced into mounting counter-attacks or a major pre-emptive strike to save itself from what al-Ayubi calls "moral attrition." Therefore, he says, the Arabs require a highly mobile shield of aircraft, armor, mechanized infantry and missiles in such measure that Israel would be deterred from counter-attacks. Should the Israelis indeed attempt to penetrate this massive shield, the Arabs would switch tactics, attacking deep into Israeli territory but "staging a strategic retreat after the strike and before American intervention."

Al-Ayubi, a thorough man, goes into great detail and considers all pertinent factors from psychology to geography. His goal is no different from that of Sadat. He, too, uses the term "withering away." His strategy, he believes, would make the Israelis realize that "the country which Zionism intended to provide a safe and secure spot for the Jews of the world has become, instead, their most dangerous spot." He expects that out of the implementation of his war plan the conviction will take root in Israel that "the racist military solution is on the verge of doom" and that the moment is at hand for the establishment of a "democratic Middle East state . . . which will be a true cultural outlet upon the shores of the Mediterranean."

It is not necessary to adopt all the convolutions of al-

Ayubi's plan in order to strive for the creation through war of a true cultural outlet on the Mediterranean. Without argument, the Arab world accepts the basic premise, *i.e.* that there will have to be a series of military campaigns to wear Israel down until the Israelis understand the hopelessness of further resistance. The thought is always present that, in the fifth round or the sixth or the seventh, the Arab armies will at last break the Israeli lines and, moving too swiftly for the Americans to intervene, sweep to the shores of Tel Aviv and the heights of Haifa's Mount Carmel.

There is no brilliance here, merely the wisdom that comes from accumulated experience. Experience, particularly in 1973, taught the Arabs that high wartime casualties create an almost unbearable trauma in a people bled of the best of its youth in four wars. Experience—in 1956, 1967, 1973—taught the Arabs that weapons which the Arabs lose in war can easily be replaced courtesy of Soviet policy and/ or the Western market economy, whereas Israeli arms supplies depend on American whims, and Israel must sometimes pay a high political price for new weapons. Experience—1956, 1973—taught the Arabs that the superpowers will not tolerate an overwhelming Arab defeat and will, instead, force the advancing Israelis into accepting a militarily premature cease-fire. Experience—particularly 1973— taught the Arabs that a long war is a far greater drain on a modern industrial country such as Israel than on underdeveloped and unsophisticated economies such as Egypt's and Syria's.

It was out of such thoughts, together with the battle lessons of the 1973 War, that Arab plans for the fifth round of warfare have evolved. William Beecher, the *Boston Globe*'s military specialist and former Information Chief at the Pentagon, concluded after a regional tour in mid-1976, that Egypt's war plan again called for a surprise attack across the Sinai. The armored sweep would not aim to capture any particular strongpoints but to advance as far as possible and, more important, to kill as many Israelis as possible. Hurriedly, building fortified positions stretching back to the original strike-out line, Egypt would then defend these positions against a presumed Israeli attack. The Egyptian plan provides for the surrender of one position after another but not before full use is made of surface-to-air missiles, anti-tank missiles, tanks and artillery. Egypt would be ready to accept a ratio of ten to twenty Egyptian dead for every Israeli killed. (The network of electronic listening-posts in Sinai, established as a result of the second disengagement accord, was designed to provide tactical early-warning, not to stop a large-scale attack, and the U.S. technicians on the spot were pledged to leave in case of real trouble.)

The plan was drafted at a point when relations with Syria were strained and it did not seem to take into account any Syrian contribution to the fifth round. The Syrians, for their part, had made such geo-strategic progress that, for the first time, they could plan for the opening of an eastern front, with Jordanian cooperation—and without the certainty of a coordinated Egyptian assault. In responding to an attack from the north and the east, the Syrian command knew, the Israelis would have to keep a large force in reserve to guard the Egyptian front. And old Middle East hands were convinced that prestige and power factors would soon compel Cairo to join any Syrian-inaugurated war. Indeed, the 1973 precedent demonstrated that all the major Arab owners of sophisticated weaponry and trained units—from Algeria through Libya to Saudi Arabia—would join the crusade. Since the eastern front, unlike the Sinai, is within easy striking distance of key Israeli civilian targets, the goal would be conquest—but also the draining of Israeli life and substance.

As the conflict in Lebanon has shown, war in the Middle

East is changing its guise with astonishing rapidity. Atrocity, once limited to extremists, has entered the language and the practice of the Average Man's battle. There were very few prisoners in Lebanon, not because none were taken, but because the captives were put to death, often slowly. In a society in which war becomes a sanctified duty, and murder a heroic act, few voices are raised against killing for the sake of killing. It is not surprising that nerve gas is part of the new Egyptian arsenal or that Israel has ordered gas masks for each of its citizens and was reported developing a gas-filtering tent to protect infants too small to be fitted with masks.

The fifth round would be a terrible war. There is a fearsome new technology awaiting testing, and the Arabs have already indicated that they have practical uses for the missile-launching sites they have set—with the aid of great powers—within range of Israel's cities. Nerve gas, biological warfare, other forms of chemical warfare are by no means contra-indicated. That the Egyptians anticipated what they were themselves planning was made obvious in 1973: the Israelis found Russian-manufactured, gas-defense equipment among the booty taken in the Sinai. There is a body of evidence that Egypt first used mustard gas against fellow Arabs, in its pointless war in Yemen in the early 1960s, dropping canisters from low-flying planes. In the next round with Israel, nerve gas could travel nearly two hundred miles in the warheads of Russian-made Scud missiles.

Also awaiting trial by combat is an impressive arsenal of other weapons which work by push-buttons and sensors. The fifth round would involve weird and/or frightful weapons, from pilotless, drone aircraft to phosphorus bombs. Casualties would be unspeakably heavy.

Israel is a country founded by refugees. For thirty years

these people have lived under siege. The men of their citizens' army have interrupted their lives time and again to go off to war, or defend the land against threats of war, for months at a time. Their cities have been shelled, their schools and markets attacked, their streets and buses booby-trapped, their sons and daughters killed and maimed, their society scarred and their economy twisted by endless war. Their lives have been blighted by Arab enemies who say without shame or embarrassment that they seek Israel's extinction as a state and as a people. It has taken almost superhuman discipline for this population to maintain its democratic structure and its humanity over the years. It is, in spite of all the bloodshed and the crushing pressures, a democratic state. It has no death penalty for murder, nor for murder by terror from outside. It reserves its death penalty for one crime alone: genocide. It does this because it is a country formed by people who know that genocide is a reality.

The Arabs have already fulfilled al-Ayubi's first prophecy: Israel is indeed the most dangerous spot in the world for the Jews. Nothing in Israel's recent history, however, indicates that they are ready to submit to the sort of war that al-Ayubi envisages or the process which Anwar el-Sadat describes.

For there is the threat of genocide—nothing less—when 20 nations numbering 150 million people combine to attack a single state of 3 million, determining beforehand to accept 10 to 20 times as many killed—or similar mad ratios—as their enemy. In such a war, the Cause is not Palestine, or refugees, or territories, or lost pride, or the mystical unity of the Arab Nation; it is killing.

Inevitably, unless the civilized world moves to forestall it, there will be another terrible bloodletting in the Middle East. It will be fueled by concessions to the Arabs by sycophantic nations; implemented with arms supplied by France, Britain, the Soviet Union, even the People's Republic of China, but most of all by the United States; financed by billions made through the sale of oil; supported by boycott and blackmail. And if it succeeds, it will be because the West, which knew better, did not care enough.

At the end, if they win, the Arabs will have what they want, what they preach, what they believe in: an area stretching from the Atlantic to the Indian Ocean in which no nation but a totalitarian state is of value, no culture but the Arab granted respect, no people but the Arabs entitled to full equality under the law, no law but the fist.

The Israelis, a people, as the Arabs have aptly observed, in love with life, can be expected to fight for survival as a free nation with a fierce determination equal to that of the Arabs. In essence, however, survival for Israel depends on the balance of power, power when used in war, power as a deterrent against war. And logic dictates that the time must come when the skills, courage and tactical brilliance of an army maintained by a nation 3 million strong will be outmatched by the sheer weight and volume of the arms and men under arms which a veritable world of 150 million people, emboldened and enriched by oil, pampered by the world, can amass. A raid to rescue hijacked Jews may raise Israeli morale but has no effect on the cold statistics of strategic power, halts no arms sales to the Arabs, changes no power alignments. A civil war in Lebanon weakens and divides the Arabs temporarily, but they have the resources to recuperate in time and the ability, when required, to coalesce again.

It is not surprising, then, that the question of the ultimate weapon arises periodically. For years, pundits, analysts, journalists have speculated as to whether Israel does or does not possess The Bomb. The best judgment in the intelligence community at this writing is: No, but Israel *could* build The Bomb. Israel has the human and material where-withal to make an atomic bomb, Israel possesses delivery systems capable of carrying The Bomb to target. Writing in a periodical of the respected International Institute for Strategic Studies, a British scholar concluded in 1975: "Is-rael's potential for an atomic arsenal is almost beyond dis-pute." This is known, in think-tank jargon, as "maintaining the nuclear option." Israel is generally viewed as one of a half dozen or so industrial nations maintaining that option; it is the only nation among them whose survival is chal-lenged.

Jerusalem's official position has remained unchanged from crisis to crisis: Israel will not be the first to introduce atomic weapons into the Middle East. But as the pressures on Israel grew after the Yom Kippur War, so grew the pres-sures within Israel to exercise the option, to build The Bomb as a deterrent. The arguments were powerful: the crushing burden of the arms race, the potential dangers and costs of a new Arab assault, the deep fear that Israeli de-pendence on America for conventional weapons might lead to irresistible demands from Washington for an Israeli re-treat to the point of national impotence. Former Defense Minister Moshe Dayan has lent his prestige to the case for a nuclear deterrent. Perhaps the most eloquent argument, however, came from Ephraim Kishon, Israel's Will Rogers, a political and social satirist whose sharp pen often cap-tures the mood of the Israeli public. "Our one and only al-ternative to destruction by arms race is to develop a nuclear deterrent of our own," he wrote in a column in the popular afternoon daily, *Ma'ariv*, in mid-1976. "Sooner or later we'll have to say it out loud. Sooner or later we'll have to announce: If any Arab army crosses this green line we re-serve the right to use atomic weapons, and if it crosses the

THE PLOT TO DESTROY ISRAEL

red line we'll drop the bomb automatically, even if this whole country is blown up by nuclear retaliation. You don't believe it? Try us.''

Awesome words written in seriousness and read from one end of the country to the other.

The problem, of course, is contained in Kishon's phrase, ". . . even if this whole country is blown up by nuclear retaliation"; use of the weapon would provoke the most fearsome response, from the Soviets first of all, against a small and peculiarly vulnerable country. And as a threat in Israel's hands, The Bomb would be less than perfect; its existence in Israel's armory would provide no protection against terror, no security against guerrilla raids, no insurance against a war of attrition, no checkmate against a war of limited objectives, no guarantee against diplomatic or economic blackmail. Further, Israel's acquisition of the bomb might well persuade one or another of the members of the atomic club to line the Arabs up for membership. Nor is there such a thing as a permanent regional monopoly on nuclear technology. Courtesy of the USSR, the Arabs have A-bomb delivery systems, and, inexorably, they are moving toward development of the nuclear option themselves; in 1976 there were hundreds of students from Libya, an underdeveloped desert country which floats on a sea of oil, studying nuclear physics in the United States. Not least important, suspicion that Israel was in the process of exercising the nuclear option and constructing a deterrent weapon would act as a catalyst to compel the Arabs to thrust aside internal quarrels and to attack before the deadline.

Barring the outside chance of bold and united international action, then, there are no escapes. There is only the endless, dangerous conflict, the constant state of alert, the immutable march toward the fifth round of classic warfare and, since war knows no logic, the ever-present possibility that desperate men may take desperate steps or use desperate weapons. In no other country of the contemporary world would Kishon's words have made a kind of sense.

The superpowers were thoroughly enmeshed in the fourth round. They could hardly avoid involvement in a fifth and much more perilous round of war. The threat of Armageddon, the final battle, would be potent.

In the Yom Kippur War, Frog missiles fell in the Galilee not far from Har Meggido, the ancient battleground whose name has been transmuted to Armageddon. The dangers and implications of a fifth round defy description. But the Book of Revelation provides a word-portrait of the final battle which, perhaps, will be warning enough: "And they gathered them together at the place which is called in Hebrew, Armageddon. . . . And there were flashes of lightning, loud noises, peals of thunder, and a great earthquake, such as had never been since men were on the earth, so great was that earthquake . . . and the cities of the nations fell. . . . And every island fled away, and no mountains were to be found, and great hailstones, heavy as a hundredweight, dropped on men from heaven, till men cursed God for the plague of the hail, so fearful was that plague."

Epilogue

Short weeks before the accession of the Carter Administration, the Arabs mounted a new campaign in their war of destruction against Israel. The catch-word this time was Peace. The major weapon in the "peace offensive" was oil. In return for its generosity in holding an oil-price increase to "only" five percent, Saudi Arabia expected the United States to show "appreciation" by forcing an Arab-style peace on Israel.

The blackmail was softened by images of new moderation in which none other than Yasir Arafat, the angel of the Lebanese war, figured prominently. The PLO was to "accept" a mini-state linking the West Bank with Gaza via a corridor slicing through Israel.

Were the pivotal Arab states, then, ready for peace? No. They were ready, as Anwar el-Sadat acknowledged, to repay Israel for full-scale retreat with nothing more than an end to "the state of war," without open frontiers, trade or diplomatic relations. Israel would thus remain, as she had been for three decades, the pariah of the Middle East, but added to her isolation would be a new vulnerability and the presence of a new Arab state called Palestine, a state viewed by the Arab world simply as a step toward Israel's elimination.

What if Israel refused to sign her own death warrant? Hafez el-Assad, with Sadat one of the world's newfound "moderates," had an easy answer; there was always, he pointed out in the midst of the "peace offensive," the "military option."

Index

249

255